Essentials

W9-APK-028

of PSYCHOLOGICAL ASSESSMENT *Series*

Everything you need to know to administer, interpret, and score the major psychological tests.

I'd like to order the following
ESSENTIALS OF PSYCHOLOGICAL ASSESSMENT:

- ❏ **WAIS®-III Assessment / 28295-2 / $34.95**
- ❏ **CAS Assessment / 29015-7 / $34.95**
- ❏ **Millon Inventories Assessment / 29798-4 / $34.95**
- ❏ **Forensic Psychological Assessment / 33186-4 / $34.95**
- ❏ **Bayley Scales of Infant Development-II Assessment / 32651-8 / $34.95**
- ❏ **Myers-Briggs Type Indicator® Assessment / 33239-9 / $34.95**
- ❏ **WISC-III® and WPPSI-R® Assessment / 34501-6 / $34.95**
- ❏ **Career Interest Assessment / 35365-5 / $34.95**
- ❏ **Rorschach® Assessment / 33146-5 / $34.95**
- ❏ **Cognitive Assessment with KAIT and Other Kaufman Measures 38317-1 / $34.95**
- ❏ **MMPI-2™ Assessment / 34533-4 / $34.95**
- ❏ **Nonverbal Assessment / 38318-X / $34.95**
- ❏ **Cross-Battery Assessment / 38264-7 / $34.95**
- ❏ **NEPSY® Assessment / 32690-9 / $34.95**
- ❏ **Individual Achievement Assessment / 32432-9/$34.95**
- ❏ **TAT and Other Storytelling Techniques Assessment / 39469-6 / $34.95**

Please send this order form with your payment (credit card or check) to:
JOHN WILEY & SONS, INC., Attn: J. Knott, 10th Floor
605 Third Avenue, New York, N.Y. 10158-0012

Name _____

Affiliation _____

Address _____

City/State/Zip _____

Phone _____ E-mail _____

❏ Would you like to be added to our e-mailing list?

Credit Card: ❏ MasterCard ❏ Visa ❏ American Express
(All orders subject to credit approval)

Card Number _____

Exp. Date _____ Signature _____

TO ORDER BY PHONE, CALL 1-800-225-5945
Refer to promo code #1-4081

Ⓦ **WILEY**

To order online: www.wiley.com/essentials

Essentials of Psychological Assessment Series
Series Editors, Alan S. Kaufman and Nadeen L. Kaufman

Essentials of WAIS®-III Assessment
by Alan S. Kaufman and Elizabeth O. Lichtenberger

Essentials of Millon Inventories Assessment
by Stephen N. Strack

Essentials of CAS Assessment
by Jack A. Naglieri

Essentials of Forensic Psychological Assessment
by Marc J. Ackerman

Essentials of Bayley Scales of Infant Development–II Assessment
by Maureen M. Black and Kathleen Matula

Essentials of Myers-Briggs Type Indicator® Assessment
by Naomi Quenk

Essentials of WISC-III® and WPPSI-R® Assessment
by Alan S. Kaufman and Elizabeth O. Lichtenberger

Essentials of Rorschach® Assessment
by Tara Rose, Nancy Kaser-Boyd, and Michael P. Maloney

Essentials of Career Interest Assessment
by Jeffrey P. Prince and Lisa J. Heiser

Essentials of Cross-Battery Assessment
by Dawn P. Flanagan and Samuel O. Ortiz

Essentials of Cognitive Assessment with KAIT and Other Kaufman Measures
by Elizabeth O. Lichtenberger, Debra Broadbooks, and Alan S. Kaufman

Essentials of Nonverbal Assessment
by Steve McCallum, Bruce Bracken, and John Wasserman

Essentials of MMPI-2™ Assessment
by David S. Nichols

Essentials of NEPSY® Assessment
by Sally L. Kemp, Ursula Kirk, and Marit Korkman

Essentials of Individual Achievement Assessment
by Douglas K. Smith

Essentials of TAT and Other Storytelling Techniques Assessment
by Hedwig Teglasi

Essentials of WJ III™ Tests of Achievement Assessment
by Nancy Mather, Barbara J. Wendling, and Richard V Woodcock

Essentials of WJ III™ Cognitive Abilities Assessment
by Fredrick A. Schrank, Dawn P. Flanagan, Richard W Woodcock, and Jennifer T. Mascolo

Essentials of WMS®-III Assessment
by Elizabeth O. Lichtenberger, Alan S. Kaufman, and Zona C. Lai

Essentials of MMPI-A™ Assessment
by Robert P. Archer and Radhika Krishnamurthy

Essentials of Neuropsychological Assessment
by Nancy Hebben and William Milberg

Essentials of Behavioral Assessment
by Michael C. Ramsay, Cecil R. Reynolds, and Randy W. Kamphaus

Essentials

of WJ III™ Cognitive
Abilities Assessment

Fredrick A. Schrank

Dawn P. Flanagan

Richard W. Woodcock

Jennifer T. Mascolo

 John Wiley & Sons, Inc.

Library of Congress Cataloging-in-Publication Data:
Essentials of WJ III cognitive abilities assessment / Fredrick A. Schrank . . . [et al.].
        p. cm. — (Essentials of psychological assessment series)
    Includes bibliographical references (p.).
    ISBN 0-471-34466-4 (pbk.)
        1. Woodcock-Johnson Tests of Cognitive Ability.   I. Schrank, Fredrick A. (Fredrick Allen)
II. Series.

    BF432.5. W66 E88 2002
    153.9'3—dc21

                                                                                2001045393

ACKNOWLEDGMENTS

Three other individuals made significant contributions to the *Essentials of WJ III Cognitive Abilities Assessment:* Krista Smart of Calgary, Alberta; Barbara Wendling of Dallas, Texas; and Carissa Kowalski of Chicago, Illinois.

CONTENTS

SERIES PREFACE

In the *Essentials of Psychological Assessment* series, we have attempted to provide the reader with books that will deliver key practical information in the most efficient and accessible style. The series features instruments in a variety of domains, such as cognition, personality, education, and neuropsychology. For the experienced clinician, books in the series will offer a concise, yet thorough way to master utilization of the continuously evolving supply of new and revised instruments, as well as a convenient method for keeping up to date on the tried-and-true measures. The novice will find here a prioritized assembly of all the information and techniques that must be at one's fingertips to begin the complicated process of individual psychological diagnosis.

Wherever feasible, visual shortcuts to highlight key points are utilized alongside systematic, step-by-step guidelines. Chapters are focused and succinct. Topics are targeted for an easy understanding of the essentials of administration, scoring, interpretation, and clinical application. Theory and research are continually woven into the fabric of each book, but always to enhance clinical inference, never to sidetrack or overwhelm. We have long been advocates of "intelligent" testing—the notion that a profile of test scores is meaningless unless it is brought to life by the clinical observations and astute detective work of knowledgeable examiners. Test profiles must be used to make a difference in the child's or adult's life, or why bother to test? We want this series to help our readers become the best intelligent testers they can be.

In *Essentials of WJ III™ Cognitive Abilities Assessment,* the authors provide a concise primer in *WJ III Tests of Cognitive Abilities* administration, scoring and interpretation. In addition, they go beyond the material already available in the WJ III manuals to provide a unique perspective on the history and clinical applications of the WJ III for the assessment of individuals with learning disabilities.

Alan S. Kaufman, PhD, and Nadeen L. Kaufman, EdD, Series Editors
Yale University School of Medicine

One

The Woodcock-Johnson III Tests of Cognitive Abilities (WJ III COG; Woodcock, McGrew, & Mather, 2001c) is a battery of carefully engineered tests for measuring cognitive abilities and related aspects of cognitive functioning (Woodcock, 1992). The WJ III COG was conormed with the Woodcock-Johnson III Tests of Achievement (WJ III ACH; Woodcock, McGrew, & Mather, 2001b) to form the complete Woodcock-Johnson III (WJ III; Woodcock, McGrew, & Mather, 2001a). Using the WJ III COG and the WJ III ACH together, professionals can make accurate comparisons among an individual's cognitive abilities, oral language ability, and achievement scores. Some WJ III COG tests are appropriate for individuals as young as 24 months, and all of the tests can be used with individuals from 5 to 95 years of age. Special norms are provided for college and university students.

The WJ III COG is based on the *Cattell-Horn-Carroll (CHC) theory of cognitive abilities*. All three strata of CHC theory are represented in the WJ III COG. Although the primary purpose of the WJ III COG is to provide professionals with accurate measurement of the broad CHC factor scores (stratum II), the battery also provides a first-principle component general ability score (g) as a measure of general intellectual ability (stratum III). Additionally, the individual cognitive tests are distinctive measures of many of the narrow abilities defined by CHC theory (stratum I).

This book is intended to help you understand the essentials of intellectual ability assessment using the WJ III COG. Although interpretation of the WJ III COG can be complex, this book is presented in an easy-to-read format. Administration, scoring, and interpretation are all addressed in simple language. The clinical applications and case report chapters are intended to help you round out your clinical repertoire with practical examples and illustrations. Throughout the book, important points are highlighted by "Rapid Reference,"

"Caution," and "Don't Forget" boxes. At the end of Chapters 1–6, "Test Yourself" sections will help you assess your understanding of what you have read.

This chapter begins with a discussion of how the Woodcock-Johnson cognitive tests have evolved to become the most comprehensive battery of cognitive abilities tests available to assessment professionals. Next, the principle of
selective testing is introduced to help you determine which tests to administer.
Finally, this chapter will summarize the technical characteristics of the WJ III
COG.

HISTORY AND DEVELOPMENT

The WJ III COG represents the third generation of the cognitive tests that
originally formed Part One of the Woodcock-Johnson Psycho-Educational
Battery (WJPEB; Woodcock & Johnson, 1977). Initial work on this battery of
tests began in 1973. In 1989, the Woodcock-Johnson Psycho-Educational Battery–Revised (Woodcock & Johnson, 1989a) was published. The WJ III COG
was published in 2001.

1977: The Woodcock-Johnson Psychoeducational Battery

The WJPEB began as one battery that consisted of three parts: Tests of Cognitive Ability, Tests of Achievement, and Tests of Interest Level. Initially,
there was no overriding theoretical model that guided development of the
cognitive tests. Instead, test development consisted of a number of controlled
experiments for measuring learning abilities. The first test constructed was
Visual-Auditory Learning (Woodcock, 1958). It was developed to predict an
individual's ability to learn to read. Later, the Analysis-Synthesis test was developed to measure an individual's ability to learn mathematics. Additional
cognitive tests were developed to comprise a heterogeneous mix of broad and
complex cognitive abilities. In the end, 12 tests were included in the cognitive
portion of the battery. These tests represented both verbal and nonverbal
functions (a common interpretive construct of that time). Additionally, the
abilities sampled were designed to fall on a continuum from lower mental
processes (simple operations) to higher mental processes (complex operations).

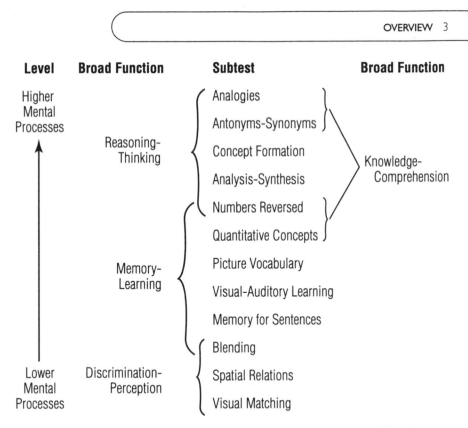

Level	Broad Function	Subtest	Broad Function

Higher Mental Processes

Lower Mental Processes

Reasoning-Thinking

Memory-Learning

Discrimination-Perception

Analogies

Antonyms-Synonyms

Concept Formation

Analysis-Synthesis

Numbers Reversed

Quantitative Concepts

Picture Vocabulary

Visual-Auditory Learning

Memory for Sentences

Blending

Spatial Relations

Visual Matching

Knowledge-Comprehension

Figure 1.1 Broad Functions, Level-of-Processing Descriptions, and Twelve Cognitive Tests from the 1977 WJPEB

Test construction followed a scientific-empirical method. Following the battery's norming (which occurred in 1976 and 1977), factor and cluster analyses were conducted to help define a small number of broad functions measured by the battery. Four functions were identified and defined: Knowledge-Comprehension, Reasoning-Thinking, Memory-Learning, and Discrimination-Perception. Figure 1.1 illustrates this model.

In the 1970s, the term *intelligence quotient* and its abbreviation, *IQ,* were viewed somewhat negatively by many people. However, an overall cognitive score was viewed as a necessity. As a consequence, the term *Broad Cognitive Ability (BCA)* was introduced. In deriving the BCA, the 12 cognitive tests were differentially weighted to give a statistically better estimate of an individual's overall cognitive ability than would be obtained by weighting the tests equally.

WJPEB Subtests	COGNITIVE FACTORS							
	Glr	*Gsm*	*Gs*	*Ga*	*Gv**	*Gc*	*Gf*	*Gq*
Visual-Auditory Learning	●							
Memory for Sentences		○				○		
Numbers Reversed		○						
Spatial Relations**			●					
Visual Matching			●					
Blending				●				
Picture Vocabulary						●		
Antonyms-Synonyms						●		
Analysis-Synthesis							●	
Concept Formation							●	
Analogies						○	○	
Quantitative Concepts								●
Word Attack				○				
Calculation								●
Applied Problems								●
Science						●		
Social Studies						●		
Humanities						●		

Glr—Long-Term Retrieval
Gsm—Short-Term Memory   ● High Loadings
Gs—Processing Speed   ○ Moderate Loadings
Ga—Auditory Processing
Gv—Visual Processing
Gc—Comprehension-Knowledge
Gf—Fluid Reasoning
Gq—Quantitative Ability

* There are no measures of Gv in the 1977 WJPEB.

** Spatial Relations is a highly speeded test in the 1977 WJPEB.

Figure 1.2 Cognitive Factors Measured by the 1977 WJPEB

1989: The Woodcock-Johnson Psychoeducational Battery–Revised

In 1985, John Horn presented a paper at a conference honoring Lloyd Humphreys. That paper fostered insight into the structure of human intellectual capabilities, and laid the theoretical foundation for the WJ-R Tests of Cognitive Ability (WJ-R COG; Woodcock & Johnson, 1989c). Subsequently, the WJ-R COG came to be described as an operational representation of *Gf-Gc* theory (Horn, 1991).

Kevin McGrew conducted much of the statistical work for the WJ-R and served as primary author of the *WJ-R Technical Manual* (McGrew, Werder, & Woodcock, 1991). Following Horn's 1985 presentation, McGrew synthesized all of the extant exploratory and confirmatory factor analyses of the 1977 WJPEB. He developed a table, similar to that found in Figure 1.2, that served as a blueprint for planning and organizing the revision to approximate *Gf-Gc* theory more closely.

Ten new tests were developed and added to the WJ-R COG. As a consequence, the WJ-R COG became the primary battery of tests for measuring seven broad abilities identified in *Gf-Gc* theory: Long-Term Retrieval (*Glr*), Short-Term Memory (*Gsm*), Processing Speed (*Gs*), Auditory Processing (*Ga*), Visual Spatial-Thinking (*Gv*), Comprehension-Knowledge (*Gc*), and Fluid Reasoning (*Gf*). An eighth factor, Quantitative Ability (*Gq*), was available when using the WJ-R Tests of Achievement (Woodcock & Johnson, 1989b). Rapid Reference 1.1 outlines these eight abilities.

Gf-Gc theory was soon applied to the analysis and interpretation of other intelligence tests. In a groundbreaking work, Woodcock (1990) showed that *Gf-Gc* theory describes the factor structure of other intelligence test batteries when their sets of tests are included in studies with sufficient breadth and depth of markers to ensure that the presence of all major factors could be identified. The paper became widely cited in psychological and educational lit-

≣ *Rapid Reference 1.1*

Eight *Gf-Gc* Abilities Measured by the 1989 WJ-R

Long-Term Retrieval (*Glr*)
Short-Term Memory (*Gsm*)
Processing Speed (*Gs*)
Auditory Processing (*Ga*)
Visual Spatial-Thinking (*Gv*)
Comprehension-Knowledge (*Gc*)
Fluid Reasoning (*Gf*)
Quantitative Ability (*Gq*)

erature. As a consequence, *Gf-Gc* theory gained support as a major descriptor of human intellectual abilities and as a standard for evaluating tests of intelligence (McGrew & Flanagan, 1998).

2001: The Woodcock-Johnson III

In 1993, John Carroll published *Human Cognitive Abilities: A Survey of Factor-Analytic Studies*. The thesis of this book is often described as Carroll's *three-stratum theory* (Carroll, 1993, 1998). The book presents the idea that we can conceptualize human cognitive abilities in a three-stratum hierarchy. Through an independent analysis of 461 data sets, Carroll identified 69 specific, or narrow, cognitive abilities (stratum I), similar to the Well Replicated Common Factor (WERCOF) abilities identified by Horn and his associates (Ekstrom, French, & Harman, 1979). In addition, Carroll grouped the narrow abilities into broad categories of cognitive abilities (stratum II) that are remarkably similar to the broad *Gf-Gc* factors described by Horn and his associates.

The overall category of Cattell-Horn-Carroll research came to be called *CHC theory*, and was used as a blueprint to build more breadth into the broad factors of the WJ III, thus providing greater generalizability (validity) of the factor scores to other situations. This was accomplished, for most factors, by creating the factor score from two or more tests of qualitatively different narrow, or stratum I, abilities. Rapid Reference 1.2 is a list of the CHC abilities measured by the WJ III COG.

Carroll identified a general intellectual ability factor (*g*) at the apex of his three-stratum model. Other scholars of intelligence, most notably Horn, do not posit *g* as an entity. However the presence of a psychometric *g* factor is not the subject of debate; *g* may merely be a statistical artifact or it may represent a quality of cognitive functioning representing a complex interplay of all abilities. Nonetheless, because many professionals have indicated a need for a general intellectual ability score on the WJ III COG, a first-principal component (*g*) score is made available. The score is called *General Intellectual Ability*, or *GIA*. The GIA score is distinct from full-scale scores provided by other intelligence tests that provide only arithmetic means of all tests or subtests contained in a particular battery.

The primary purpose of the WJ III COG is to provide measurement of the broad CHC factor scores. These broad ability scores provide important diagnostic information for analysis of within-individual variability. However, the qualita-

≋Rapid Reference 1.2

CHC Theory Abilities Measured by the WJ III COG

Stratum I	Stratum II	Stratum III
Lexical Knowledge/Language Development	Comprehension-Knowledge	General Intellectual Ability
General (verbal) Information		
Associate Memory	Long-Term Retrieval	
Ideational Fluency		
Visualization	Visual-Spatial Thinking	
Spatial Relations		
Spatial Scanning		
Speech-Sound Discrimination	Auditory Processing	
Resistance to Auditory Stimulus Distortion		
Phonetic Coding		
Induction	Fluid Reasoning	
Sequential Reasoning		
Semantic Processing Speed	Processing Speed	
Perceptual Speed		
Naming Facility		
Memory Span	Short-Term Memory	

Source: Adapted from WJ III Newsletter, p. 7, Riverside Publishing 2001.

tively different narrow abilities measured by the component tests can serve as a rich source of interpretive information in individual cases in which the tests that comprise a cluster differ significantly. Additionally, the inclusion of the GIA score increases the overall comprehensiveness of the WJ III by making a g score available.

The wide breadth of measurement in each factor is intended to provide greater validity of the CHC factor score. Because the factors have more breadth, the practical implications of cluster score performance can be generalized to more situations. In general, each broad CHC factor is composed of two qualitatively different narrow (stratum I) abilities. For example, the *Glr* cluster includes a measure of associative memory (Test 2: Visual-Auditory Learning) and a measure of ideational fluency (Test 12: Retrieval Fluency). Similarly, the *Gv* cluster includes a measure of visualization (Test 3: Spatial Relations) and a measure of visual memory (Test 13: Picture Recognition).

The WJ III COG includes eight new tests that broaden the range of abilities measured in the assessment. Rapid Reference 1.3 describes these tests.

SELECTIVE TESTING

The WJ III COG contains 20 tests, each measuring a different aspect of cognitive ability. Rarely is it necessary, or even desirable, to administer all 20 tests. Instead, you should apply the principle of *selective testing:* That is, for each individual, select the tests that will elicit the most relevant and appropriate information. Combinations of the 20 tests provide clusters that are used for interpretive purposes. The WJ III COG has two parts, the Standard Battery (Tests 1–10) and the Extended Battery (Tests 11–20). Depending on the purpose of the assessment, you may choose any combination of tests or clusters to administer. The following examples are intended to help you use the Selective Testing Table in Rapid Reference 1.4 to match specific combinations of WJ III COG tests to the purposes of the assessment.

For example, if an overall measure of intellectual functioning is needed, you may administer either the GIA–Standard (GIA-Std) or GIA–Extended (GIA-Ext) scales. The GIA-Std scale consists of seven tests—Test 1: Verbal Comprehension; Test 2: Visual-Auditory Learning; Test 3: Spatial Relations; Test 4: Sound Blending; Test 5: Concept Formation; Test 6: Visual Matching; and Test 7: Numbers Reversed. The GIA-Ext tests include all of the tests in the GIA-Std scale, plus seven tests from the Extended Battery—Test 11: General Information; Test 12: Retrieval Fluency; Test 13: Picture Recognition; Test 14: Auditory Attention; Test 15: Analysis-Synthesis; Test 16: Decision Speed; and Test 17: Memory for Words. If a brief measure of intellectual ability is desired, you should administer Test 1: Verbal Comprehension, Test 5: Concept Formation, and Test 6: Visual Matching. If a subsequent determination is made to obtain a general intellectual ability score, the additional tests that comprise the GIA-Std or GIA-Ext scales can be administered.

If you need measures of specific cognitive abilities, administer the selected tests that comprise the broad ability. Cognitive factor scores may be obtained

Rapid Reference 1.3

Descriptions of New WJ III COG Tests

Standard Battery

Test 9: Auditory Working Memory

An audio recording presents the subject with a series of unrelated digits and words. The subject is asked to repeat the words, and then the numbers, in the order in which they were presented. This test is designed to measure short-term auditory working memory span.

Extended Battery

Test 11: General Information

General Information is made up of two subtests: Where and What. In GI-Where, the subject is asked, "Where would you usually find [object]?" In GI-What, the subject is asked, "What would people usually do with [object]?" The task measures the depth of the subject's verbal knowledge.

Test 12: Retrieval Fluency

The subject is given 1 min to name as many foods or drinks as he or she can. This process is repeated with names of people and types of animals. This test measures the fluency of retrieval from stored knowledge.

Test 14: Auditory Attention

The subject is shown a row of pictures and asked to point to the one indicated by the audio recording. The audio recording incorporates increasingly distracting background noise and words that sound more and more similar. This test measures how well the subject can overcome the effects of auditory distortion or masking in understanding oral language.

Test 16: Decision Speed

Decision Speed is a timed test that requires the subject to examine a row of pictures and point out the two that are the most conceptually similar. This task is designed to measure the speed of processing simple concepts.

Test 18: Rapid Picture Naming

The subject is given 2 min to name as many pictures on the Test Book pages as he or she can. Rapid Picture Naming tests the subject's ability to recall quickly information from acquired knowledge.

Test 19: Planning

The Planning test requires the subject to trace a pattern without removing his or her pencil from the paper or retracing any lines. This complex task draws on fluid reasoning and visual processing skills.

Test 20: Pair Cancellation

In this test, the subject is asked to circle a pair of objects that is repeated throughout a page of objects; the subject is given 3 min to circle as many pairs as possible. Pair Cancellation provides information about executive processing, attention/concentration, and processing speed abilities.

≡ Rapid Reference 1.4

WJ III COG Selective Testing Table

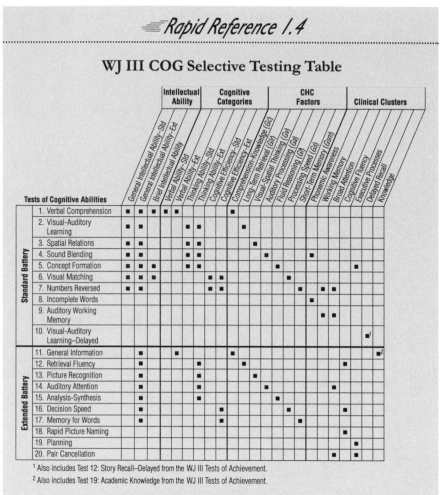

Tests of Cognitive Abilities	Intellectual Ability					Cognitive Categories				CHC Factors							Clinical Clusters						
	General Intellectual Ability–Std	General Intellectual Ability–Ext	Brief Intellectual Ability	Verbal Ability–Std	Verbal Ability–Ext	Thinking Ability–Std	Thinking Ability–Ext	Cognitive Efficiency–Std	Cognitive Efficiency–Ext	Comprehension-Knowledge (Gc)	Long-Term Retrieval (Glr)	Visual-Spatial Thinking (Gv)	Auditory Processing (Ga)	Fluid Reasoning (Gf)	Processing Speed (Gs)	Short-Term Memory (Gsm)	Phonemic Awareness	Working Memory	Broad Attention	Cognitive Fluency	Executive Processes	Delayed Recall	Knowledge
Standard Battery																							
1. Verbal Comprehension	■	■	■	■	■					■													
2. Visual-Auditory Learning	■	■				■	■				■												
3. Spatial Relations	■	■				■	■					■											
4. Sound Blending	■	■				■	■						■				■						
5. Concept Formation	■	■	■			■	■							■							■		
6. Visual Matching	■	■	■					■	■						■								
7. Numbers Reversed	■	■						■	■							■		■	■				
8. Incomplete Words													■										
9. Auditory Working Memory																		■	■				
10. Visual-Auditory Learning–Delayed																						■¹	
Extended Battery																							
11. General Information		■			■					■													■²
12. Retrieval Fluency		■					■				■									■			
13. Picture Recognition		■					■					■											
14. Auditory Attention		■					■						■						■				
15. Analysis-Synthesis		■					■							■									
16. Decision Speed		■							■						■					■			
17. Memory for Words		■							■							■							
18. Rapid Picture Naming																				■			
19. Planning																					■		
20. Pair Cancellation																			■		■		

¹ Also includes Test 12: Story Recall–Delayed from the WJ III Tests of Achievement.
² Also includes Test 19: Academic Knowledge from the WJ III Tests of Achievement.

Source: Adapted from WJ III Tests of Cognitive Abilities Standard Test Book, p. v. Riverside Publishing 2001.

to provide interpretive information for seven cognitive clusters: Comprehension-Knowledge, Long-Term Retrieval, Auditory Processing, Visual-Spatial Thinking, Fluid Reasoning, Short-Term Memory, and Processing Speed. For example, to obtain the Auditory Processing cluster score, you would administer Test 4: Sound Blending and Test 14: Auditory Attention.

Some of the tests in the WJ III COG are supplemental. When administered, the supplemental tests can be combined with other WJ III COG tests to obtain additional clusters that are often useful for interpretive purposes. These clusters include Phonemic Awareness, Working Memory, Broad Attention,

Cognitive Fluency, and Executive Processes. A Delayed Recall cluster and a Knowledge cluster can be obtained when the WJ III COG is combined with selected tests from the WJ III ACH.

Several types of comparisons among a subject's WJ III scores can help determine whether any significant strengths or weaknesses exist. These are described in Chapter 4, "How to Interpret the WJ III COG."

STANDARDIZATION AND PSYCHOMETRIC PROPERTIES OF THE WJ III COG

The WJ III norming sample was selected to be representative (within practical limits) of the U.S. population from age 24 months to age 90 years and older. The total standardization sample included 8,818 subjects. These individuals were representatively selected from more than 100 geographically and economically diverse communities. The preschool sample (2 to 5 years of age and not enrolled in kindergarten) was composed of 1,143 subjects; the kindergarten through 12th-grade sample was composed of 4,783 subjects; the college/university sample was composed of 1,165 undergraduate and graduate students; and the adult sample was composed of 1,843 subjects.

Data from the 8,818 norming subjects were summarized for each test and cluster. Age norms are provided at one-month intervals from age 2 years 0 months (2-0) to 18 years 11 months (18-11), and at one-year intervals from age 19 to 95+. Grade norms are provided at one-month intervals from K.0 to 18.0. Two-year college norms (grades 13 and 14) are also available for use with technical and community college students.

Reliability statistics were calculated for all WJ III COG tests across their range of intended use and included all norming subjects tested. The reliabilities for all but the speeded tests and tests with multiple-point scoring systems were calculated using the split-half procedure (odd and even items) and corrected for length using the Spearman-Brown correction formula. The reliabilities for the speeded tests (Visual Matching, Retrieval Fluency, Decision Speed, Rapid Picture Naming, and Pair Cancellation) and tests with multiple-point scored items (Spatial Relations, Retrieval Fluency, Picture Recognition, and Planning) were calculated using Rasch analysis procedures. Rapid Reference 1.5 reports the median reliability coefficients (r_{11}) and the standard errors of measurement (SEMs) obtained using the procedures described above. Most r_{11} numbers are .80 or higher, which is a desirable level for an individual test.

Median Test Reliability Statistics

Test	Median r_{11}	Median SEM (SS)
Standard Battery		
Test 1: Verbal Comprehension	.92	4.24
Test 2: Visual-Auditory Learning	.86	5.56
Test 3: Spatial Relations	.81	6.51
Test 4: Sound Blending	.89	5.04
Test 5: Concept Formation	.94	3.64
Test 6: Visual Matching	.91	4.60
Test 7: Numbers Reversed	.87	5.38
Test 8: Incomplete Words	.81	6.61
Test 9: Auditory Working Memory	.87	5.37
Test 10: Visual Auditory Learning–Delayed	.94	3.73
Extended Battery		
Test 11: General Information	.89	4.97
Test 12: Retrieval Fluency	.85	5.87
Test 13: Picture Recognition	.76	7.36
Test 14: Auditory Attention	.88	5.21
Test 15: Analysis-Synthesis	.90	4.74
Test 16: Decision Speed	.87	5.33
Test 17: Memory for Words	.80	6.63
Test 18: Rapid Picture Naming	.97	2.47
Test 19: Planning	.74	7.65
Test 20: Pair Cancellation	.81	6.56

Note. SEM (SS) = Standard error of measurement (in standard score units).

Source: Adapted from WJ III Technical Abstract, p. 11, Riverside Publishing 2001.

Rapid Reference 1.6 reports median reliabilities and SEMs for the clusters across their range of intended use. The SEM values are in standard score (SS) units. Most cluster reliabilities are .90 or higher.

The GIA scores exhibit the highest reliability among all scores on the WJ III.

≡Rapid Reference 1.6

Median Cluster Reliability Statistics

Test	Median r_{11}	Median SEM (SS)
Standard Battery		
General Intellectual Ability–Standard	.97	2.60
Brief Intellectual Ability	.95	3.35
Verbal Ability–Standard	.92	4.24
Thinking Ability–Standard	.95	3.35
Cognitive Efficiency–Standard	.92	4.24
Phonemic Awareness	.90	4.86
Working Memory	.91	4.50
Extended Battery		
General Intellectual Ability–Extended	.98	2.12
Verbal Ability–Extended	.95	3.35
Thinking Ability–Extended	.96	3.00
Cognitive Efficiency–Extended	.93	3.97
Comprehension-Knowledge (Gc)	.95	3.35
Long-Term Retrieval (Glr)	.88	5.20
Visual-Spatial Thinking (Gv)	.81	6.54
Auditory Processing (Ga)	.91	4.50
Fluid Reasoning (Gf)	.95	3.35
Processing Speed (Gs)	.92	4.24
Short-Term Memory (Gsm)	.88	5.20
Broad Attention	.92	4.24
Cognitive Fluency	.96	3.00
Executive Processes	.93	3.97
Delayed Recall		
Knowledge	.94	3.67
Phonemic Awareness 3	.91	4.62

Note. SEM (SS) = Standard error of measurement (in standard score units).

Source: Adapted from *WJ III Technical Abstract,* p. 12, Riverside Publishing 2001.

Both the GIA-Std and GIA-Ext scores show high internal consistency reliabilities based on the split-half procedure when corrected for length using the Spearman-Brown correction formula. The GIA-Std median reliability is .97; the median standard error of measurement in SS units is 2.60. The GIA-Ext median reliability is .98; the median standard error of measurement in SS units is 2.12.

Test-retest reliabilities were evaluated for the five speeded tests. These five tests were administered in a counter-balanced order to 165 subjects in three age-differentiated samples. The retest interval in this study was set at 1 day to minimize (but not entirely eliminate) changes in test scores due to changes in the subjects' states or traits. Rapid Reference 1.7 reports the summary statistics and test-retest reliabilities for the speeded tests.

Validity is the most important consideration in test development, evaluation, and interpretation. The WJ III COG is based on several sources of validity evidence. Content validity is addressed through mapping test and cluster content according to CHC theory. Each test was designed to be a primary measure of a narrow ability. Each of the CHC factors was designed to increase breadth of measurement by providing two qualitatively different narrow abilities subsumed in the broad ability.

The existence of divergent growth curves is one type of evidence for the exis-

≡Rapid Reference 1.7

Summary Statistics and Test-Retest Reliabilities for Five Speeded Tests

	Ages 7–11		Ages 14–17		Ages 26–79	
Test	n	r_{12}	n	r_{12}	n	r_{12}
Visual Matching	59	.87	50	.76	54	.70
Decision Speed	55	.80	48	.73	54	.73
Retrieval Fluency	59	.81	51	.85	54	.82
Rapid Picture Naming	59	.78	52	.78	53	.86
Pair Cancellation	59	.84	50	.78	52	.69
Reading Fluency	30	.94	28	.80	23	.94
Math Fluency	59	.95	52	.89	53	.96
Writing Fluency	57	.76	51	.84	53	.87

Source: Adapted from WJ III Technical Abstract, p. 13, Riverside Publishing 2001.

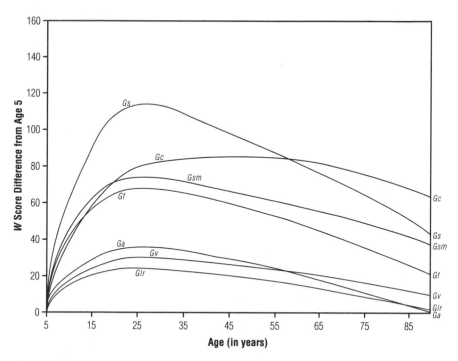

Figure 1.3 Plot of WJ III COG Growth Curves by Age

Source: Adapted from *WJ III Technical Manual*, p. 55, Riverside Publishing 2001.

tence of unique abilities (Carroll, 1983, 1993). Figure 1.3 presents the growth curves for ages 5 to 90 years for the CHC factors measured by the WJ III COG. (The examples were constructed using age 5-0 as an arbitrary starting point.) The growth curves illustrate that the unique abilities measured by the WJ III follow different developmental courses or trajectories over the age span from childhood to geriatric levels. These pictographic patterns of growth and decline are based on cross-sectional data, not longitudinal data. They portray the rise and decline of median performance across age for the general population at the time the WJ III COG was normed, not performance changes in an individual over time.

The patterns of test score intercorrelations presented in the WJ III *Technical Manual* (McGrew & Woodcock, 2001) support the interpretation of the growth curves and provide both convergent and discriminate validity evidence for the WJ III clusters. The typical range of cognitive factor intercorrelations is .20 to .60. The growth curves and intercorrelations provide support to the concept that the cognitive clusters measure intellectual abilities that are distinct from one another. Confirmatory factor analyses were also used to demonstrate that the relationships among the WJ III tests conform to the narrow ability, broad ability, and general intellectual ability strata derived from CHC theory.

In other checks of validity, the WJ III COG scores were compared to scores obtained by the same individuals on other intelligence tests. Of particular interest are the correlations between the WJ III GIA scores and the full-scale or composite scores of other intelligence batteries. Correlations with the Wechsler Intelligence Scale for Children–Third Edition (WISC-III; Wechsler, 1991) are reported as .71 for GIA-Std and .76 for GIA-Ext. Correlations with the Differential Ability Scales (DAS; Elliott, 1990) General Conceptual Ability (GCA) are similar. These correlations are reported as .76 for both GIA-Std and GIA-Ext. Results of a study with the Stanford-Binet Intelligence Scale, Fourth Edition (SB-IV; Thorndike, Hagen, & Sattler, 1986) at the preschool level show correlations with the overall composite score to be .76 for GIA-Std and .71 for the GIA-Ext. Correlations in this range are similar to those between full-scale or composite scores of other major intelligence batteries, as reported in other publications and test manuals. These correlations support the interpretation of the WJ III GIA first-principal component (g)scores as valid measures of general intellectual ability. Supporting its use as a screening measure of intellectual ability, the Brief Intellectual Ability score had correlations ranging from .60 to .70 with the Wechsler Preschool and Primary Scale of Intelligence–Revised (WPPSI-R), the WISC-III, the Wechsler Adult Intelligence Scale–Third Edition (WAIS-III; Wechsler, 1997), the DAS, the Das•Naglieri Cognitive Assessment System (CAS; Naglieri & Das, 1997), and the SB-IV. These correlations are reported in Rapid Reference 1.8.

COMPREHENSIVE REFERENCES ON THE WJ III COG

The WJ III Tests of Cognitive Abilities *Examiner's Manual* (Mather & Woodcock, 2001) provides detailed information about administering, scoring, and interpreting the WJ III COG. The WJ III *Technical Manual* provides comprehensive information about development, standardization, norming, and reliability and validity of the WJ III. Clinical applications of the WJ III COG are discussed in a book edited by Schrank and Flanagan, *WJ III Clinical Use and Interpretation* (in press). Topics in this book include assessment of individuals with learning disabilities, neuropsychological problems, Attention-Deficit Hyperactivity Disorder, and giftedness, as well as assessment of young/preschool children and individuals from different linguistic and cultural backgrounds. Rapid Reference 1.9 provides basic information on the WJ III COG and its publishers.

≡Rapid Reference 1.8

Correlations from Several Criterion Validity Studies for the General Intellectual Ability (GIA) and Brief Intellectual Ability (BIA) Scores

Criterion	Median Correlations		
	GIA-Std	GIA-Ext	BIA
Differential Ability Scales	.72	.74	.68
Wechsler Preschool and Primary Scale of Intelligence–Revised	.73	.74	.67
Stanford-Binet Intelligence Scale– Fourth Edition	.76	.71	.60
Wechsler Intelligence Scale for Children– Third Edition	.71	.76	.69
Wechsler Adult Intelligence Scale	.67	—	.62
Kaufman Adolescent and Adult Intelligence Test	.75	—	.68
Das•Naglieri Cognitive Assessment System	—	—	.70

Source: Adapted from WJ III Technical Abstract, p. 19, Riverside Publishing 2001.

≡Rapid Reference 1.9

Woodcock-Johnson III Tests of Cognitive Abilities

Authors: Richard W. Woodcock, Kevin S. McGrew, Nancy Mather

Publication Date: 2001

What the Test Measures: General Intellectual Ability (g); Comprehension-Knowledge (lexical knowledge/language development, general [verbal] information); Long-Term Retrieval (associative memory, ideational fluency); Auditory Processing (speech-sound discrimination, resistance to auditory stimulus distortion, phonetic coding); Visual-Spatial Thinking (visualization, spatial relations, spatial scanning); Fluid Reasoning (induction, sequential reasoning); Short-Term Memory (memory span); and Processing Speed (semantic processing speed, perceptual speed, naming facility); Phonemic Awareness; Working Memory; Cognitive Fluency; Broad Attention (selective attention, sustained attention, divided attention, and attentional capacity); and Executive Processes (planning, shifting, proactive interference control)

Administration Time: Varies; approximately 5 min per test

Qualification of Examiners: Graduate-level training in cognitive assessment

Publisher: Riverside Publishing Company
425 Spring Lake Dr.
Itasca, IL 60143
(800) 767-8420
www.Riverpub.com

Price: Complete test kit $575.00 without carrying case; $650 with carrying case (2001 prices)

1. The WJ III COG is based on the Cattell-Horn-Carroll (CHC) theory of human cognitive abilities. True or False?

2. Which of the following was the first Woodcock-Johnson test developed?

   (a) Analysis-Synthesis

   (b) Visual-Auditory Learning

   (c) Picture Vocabulary

   (d) Visual Matching

3. Which of the following was *not* a factor measured by the 1989 Woodcock-Johnson–Revised?

   (a) Long-Term Retrieval (*Glr*)

   (b) Fluid Reasoning (*Gf*)

   (c) Correct Decision Speed (*CDS*)

   (d) Processing Speed (*Gs*)

4. Who is credited with developing the three-stratum theory of human cognitive abilities?

   (a) Raymond Cattell

   (b) John Horn

   (c) John Carroll

   (d) Elaine Crampfoot

5. What is the age range for the WJ III COG?

   (a) 4–90 years

   (b) 5–18 years

   (c) 2–90+ years

   (d) 5–23 years

6. What was the total standardization sample size for the WJ III COG?

   (a) 4,783

   (b) 8,818

   (c) 9,000+

   (d) 6,359

7. What is the reported range of correlation between the WJ III GIA and the WISC III Full-Scale IQ?

   (a) .71–.76

   (b) .60–.70

   (c) .73–.74

   (d) .68–.75

Answers: 1. True; 2. b; 3. c; 4. c; 5. c; 6. b; 7. a

Two

HOW TO ADMINISTER THE WJ III COG

Tests such as the WJ III COG require examiners who are both skilled and patient. The validity and reliability of the test depend on the examiner's ability to accurately and consistently replicate the structure of the test as given to the norming sample. To do this, it is important to be comfortable interacting with the subject and the testing materials themselves. Although the administration procedures for the WJ III COG are not unduly complex, they do require advance preparation and participation on the part of the examiner. The best way for you to become familiar with the WJ III COG is to practice administering the tests. This chapter will give you a head start in this process by providing information about the testing materials, general assessment procedures, and test-by-test administration instructions.

TEST PREPARATION

When administering the WJ III COG tests, you should strive to be precise and brief. Practice administering the test several times to familiarize yourself with the testing formats and procedures. The testing might proceed slowly at first, but make sure to follow the instructions and script exactly until the administration becomes more fluent. After the initial practice sessions, try to maintain a brisk testing pace. A rapid testing pace, without interruptions, will shorten administration time and keep the subject from becoming restless or uninterested in the test.

The first page after the tab for each test in the Test Book provides general information and instructions specific to that test. Review this information frequently. This page usually includes scoring information, suggested starting points, basal and ceiling requirements, and information about the materials required to administer the test.

The examiner pages also include specific information on item administration. The directions include the script to be read to the subject (printed in bold blue type) and pointing instructions, if applicable. Always use the *exact* wording and instructions presented in the Test Book. The examiner pages may also include boxes with supplemental administration and scoring information.

Testing Materials

To administer the WJ III COG, you will need the following materials: the Test Books, the corresponding Test Record and Subject Response Booklet, and at least two sharpened pencils with erasers. For tests requiring an audio presentation, audio equipment—preferably with headphones—and the audio recording are also needed. For timed tests, you will need either a stopwatch, a digital watch, or a watch or clock with a second-hand. Scoring the WJ III COG requires the use of the WJ III Compuscore and Profiles Program (Schrank & Woodcock, 2001), a computer software program that is included with each WJ III COG kit. More about the specific use of these materials is included later in this book.

Setting up the Testing Area

Select a testing room that is quiet, comfortable, and has adequate ventilation and lighting. If possible, you and the subject should be the only two people in the room. The room should have a table (or other flat working surface) and two chairs, one being an appropriate size for the subject. The best seating arrangement is one in which you and the subject sit diagonally across from each other at one corner of the table. In any case, the seating arrangement should allow you to view the subject's test page and the examiner's page, point to all parts on the subject's page and the Subject Response Booklet, operate the audio equipment, and record responses out of the subject's view. The subject should be able to view only the subject pages. When the Test Book easel is set up for administration, it becomes a screen allowing the examiner to record responses on the Test Record out of the subject's view. When equipment such as the stopwatch or audio equipment is not in use, place it out of the subject's sight.

Establishing Rapport

In most instances, you will have little difficulty establishing a good relationship with the subject. Do not begin testing unless the person seems relatively comfortable with the testing situation. If he or she does not feel well or will not respond appropriately, do not attempt testing. One way of establishing rapport is to begin the testing session with a short period of conversation while you complete the "Identifying Information" portion of the Test Record. You may also preface the test using the "Introducing the Test" section that is provided in the front of each Test Book to help make the subject feel more at ease.

Smile frequently throughout the testing session and call the person by name. Between tests, let the subject know that he or she is doing a good job, using such comments as "fine" and "good." Encourage a response even when items are difficult. Be careful that any comments you make do not reveal the answers as correct or incorrect—do not say "good" only after correct responses, or pause longer after incorrect responses before proceeding to the next item.

GENERAL TESTING INFORMATION

Basal and Ceiling Criteria

Many of the WJ III COG tests require you to establish a *basal* and a *ceiling*. The purpose of basal and ceiling requirements is to limit the number of items administered but still be able to estimate, with high probability, the score that would have been obtained if all items had been administered. Eliminating the items that would be too easy or too difficult for the subject also serves to minimize testing time while maximizing the subject's tolerance for the testing situation.

Basal and ceiling criteria are included in the Test Book for each test that requires them. For some tests, subjects begin with Item 1 and continue until they reach the ceiling level; these tests do not require a basal. When administering a test with items arranged in groups or sets, the basal criterion is met when the subject correctly responds to the three consecutive lowest-numbered items in a group. If a subject fails to meet the basal criterion for any test, proceed by testing backward until the subject has met the basal criterion or you have administered Item 1.

The best practice is to test by complete pages when stimulus material appears on the subject's side of the Test Book. If a subject reaches a ceiling in the middle of a page and there is no stimulus material on the subject's page, you may discontinue testing. In this way, the subjects do not see any additional testing material and are essentially unaware that there are other items on the test.

Test Observations

Although the WJ III COG tests are designed to provide accurate quantitative information about a subject's abilities, it is also important that you observe and record the subject's reactions and behaviors in a test-taking situation. The "Test Session Observations Checklist," located on the Test Record, can help you document these observations. The checklist includes seven categories: level of conversational proficiency, level of cooperation, level of activity, attention and concentration, self-confidence, care in responding, and response to difficult tasks. Use the checklist immediately after the testing session, marking only one response for each category and noting any other clinically interesting behaviors. If the category does not apply to the individual, leave that item blank.

The checklist is designed so that a "typical" rating in each category is easily identified. For example, typical subjects are cooperative during the examination, seem at ease and comfortable, are attentive to the tasks, respond promptly but carefully, and generally persist with difficult tasks. Remember that what is typical for one age or grade level may not be typical for another; you should be familiar with the behaviors that are exhibited by specific age and grade groups. For some age or grade levels, ratings such as "appeared fidgety or restless at times" could be included within the range of behaviors deemed "typical for age/grade," rather than in a separate category.

Be sure to answer the question "Do you have any reason to believe this testing session may not represent a fair sample of the subject's abilities?" located after the checklist on the Test Record. If you check "Yes," continue by completing this sentence: "These results may not be a fair estimate because _____." Examples of reasons for questioning validity include suspected or known problems with hearing or vision, emotional problems that interfere with the subject's concentration, and certain background factors (e.g., a case in which English is not a well-established second language).

Accommodations

The WJ III COG was designed to be useful with individuals from a wide range of abilities and backgrounds. Several administration features of the WJ III COG allow individuals with disabilities to participate more fully in the evaluation process. To minimize distractability, you should use a separate room for test administration, incorporating noise buffers, special lighting, special acoustics, and/or special furniture as necessary. You may take frequent breaks and even spread the testing procedure out over several days to maximize interest and performance. With the exception of tests that are intended to measure processing speed or fluency, you may also allow additional time for subjects to complete the testing tasks. The oral instructions have been kept at a sufficiently simple level of complexity and vocabulary to avoid language comprehension barriers. These instructions may be repeated verbally (or signed, for hearing-impaired subjects) as necessary. The use of large print, fewer items per page, and increased space between items helps prevent subjects from being overwhelmed by the test pages. Visual magnification devices and templates to reduce glare can also be incorporated into the assessment without affecting validity. Audio-recorded tests may be amplified and presented at a volume that is comfortable for the subject.

Accommodations should be made only to "minimize the impact of test-taker attributes that are not relevant to the construct that is the primary focus of the assessment" (American Educational Research Association [AERA], American Psychological Association [APA], & National Council on Measurement in Education [NCME], 1999, p. 101). Because of the standardized nature of the WJ III COG, modifications to the testing procedure can fundamentally alter the results and validity of the tests. If possible, try to select tests that do not require modifications. Make note of any deviations from the standardized administration on the Test Record. In addition, always include a statement of the modified testing conditions in the Summary and Score Report produced by the Compuscore and Profiles Program.

The broad classes of subjects often requiring some type of accommodation in the assessment process are young children; English-language learners; individuals with attentional and learning difficulties; and individuals with hearing, visual, or physical impairments. When testing an individual with special needs, you should consult a trained professional with expertise in that particular area.

For a subject with a hearing impairment, this may mean hiring a certified sign-language interpreter; for a subject with Attention-Deficit Hyperactivity Disorder, it may mean speaking with a clinical expert about the nature of the disorder. In any case, it is essential that you be sensitive to the limitations that different impairments or conditions may place on a subject's abilities and behavior.

Tests Using the Subject Response Booklet

The Subject Response Booklet includes test material that the subject uses to complete tests requiring written responses. The exception is Visual Matching 2, which is located in the Test Record. Decision Speed, Planning, and Pair Cancellation require the use of the Subject Response Booklet for administration. You should provide the subject with the booklet and a sharpened pencil with an eraser when directed to do so in the Test Book. At the end of each test, collect the pencil and booklet immediately.

Tests Using the Audio Recording

Use the standardized audio recording to present Sound Blending, Numbers Reversed, Incomplete Words, Auditory Working Memory, Auditory Attention, and Memory for Words. When administering these tests, you should use good-quality audio equipment and headphones. The audio equipment must have a good speaker, be in good working order, and produce a faithful, clear reproduction of the test items.

Although some tests may be presented orally, it is recommended that you use the audio recording and headphones unless the subject resists wearing headphones or has difficulty paying attention to the audio-recorded presentation. If a test must be presented orally, attempt to say each item in the same manner that it is presented on the audio recording. You should note that Auditory Attention cannot be administered without the use of the audio recording.

If possible, you should use audio equipment with a built-in counter that can help you accurately cue-up the desired starting point for each test. By starting the recording at the beginning, you can determine the point at which each test starts and then determine the counter reading for each suggested starting point. Record these numbers in the spaces provided in the introductory section of each audio-recorded test in the Test Book.

Before you begin testing, adjust the volume of the headphones to a comfortable level for the subject. Make sure the audio recording is set to start at the correct item for that subject's level of testing. You can wear a monaural earphone or wear only one headphone over one ear to monitor the audio recording while the subject is also listening through his or her headphones. Generally, when administering an audio-recorded test, look away from the subject while the test item is being presented. After the double beep, look at the subject expectantly.

The audio recording was designed to give adequate time between items for the subject to respond. With the exception of Auditory Attention, you may stop or pause the audio recording if the subject needs additional time.

Timed Tests

Several of the WJ III COG tests are timed, including Visual Matching, Retrieval Fluency, Decision Speed, Rapid Picture Naming, and Pair Cancellation. The time limits for each timed test are indicated in the Test Book and Test Record. A stopwatch is preferred for administering these tests; however, a digital watch or a watch or clock with a second-hand may also be used if a stopwatch is not available. It is important that you monitor the time used by the subject for a test. If the subject finishes early, you must enter the exact finishing time in minutes and seconds on the Test Record. A watch or clock with a second-hand may also be useful for administering tests that have instructions to proceed if the subject has not responded within a specified period of time.

TEST-BY-TEST ADMINISTRATION PROCEDURES

Allow 45 to 50 min to administer the tests in the Standard Battery, or 1.5 to 1.75 hr to administer the tests in the complete Battery. Very young subjects or individuals with unique learning patterns may require more time.

In most cases, WJ III COG tests should be administered in the order that they appear in the easel Test Books, beginning with the Standard Battery. However, you may administer the tests in any order deemed appropriate and discontinue testing at any time. Keep in mind that the tests have been organized to alternate between different formats (e.g., timed versus untimed) to achieve optimal attention and interest.

As a general rule for all WJ III COG tests, do not penalize the subject for mispronunciations resulting from articulation errors, dialect variations, or regional speech patterns. When testing English-dominant bilingual individuals on Test 1: Verbal Comprehension, Test 11: General Information, Test 12: Retrieval Fluency, and Test 18: Rapid Picture Naming, give credit for correct answers given in either English or another language. For a few tests, such as Verbal Comprehension and General Information, examples of correct Spanish responses are provided in brackets. If the subject responds in a different language and you are unsure whether the answer is correct or incorrect, attempt to record the response for later analysis and determination.

The correct and incorrect keys in the Test Books are intended to be guides to demonstrate how certain responses are scored. Not all possible responses are included in these keys, and you may have to use your professional judgment in determining an item's score. In cases where the subject's response does not fall clearly in either the correct or incorrect category, you may wish to write down the response and come back to it later. Do not use an unscored item in determining a basal or ceiling. If, after further consideration, it is still not clear how to score several items, balance the scores by scoring one item 1 and the other item 0. If you have several questionable responses, you should seek advice from a professional colleague who may be able to help you make a determination.

If a subject asks for more information, use your judgment as to whether it is appropriate to answer his or her question. If a subject requests information that cannot be supplied, respond by saying something like, "I'm not supposed to help you with that." Even after testing has been completed, do not tell the subject whether his or her answers were correct or incorrect.

On the other hand, you may have to query the subject on certain items when his or her response is not clear. Some items in the Test Books have query keys that provide questions for specific examinee responses; use professional judgment when querying responses that do not appear in these keys. If the correctness of a response is still unclear following a query, the response should be recorded as given and scored after the testing session.

When an examinee provides multiple responses to an item requiring a single response, the general principle to follow is to *score the last answer given.* The last response, regardless of its correctness, is used to determine the final item score. This procedure should be followed even if the examinee changes an earlier response much later in the testing session. In situations where the subject provides two conflicting answers , you should query the response by asking the question "Which one?" or directing the subject to "Give just one answer."

Following are descriptions of the WJ III COG tests and their administration procedures. The tests are organized by format in order to help you learn similar equipment and testing protocols all at one time. The Rapid Reference boxes pertaining to each test description provide key information about the test, including starting point, equipment needed, and basal/ceiling criteria. A Caution box lists common examiner errors in administering the tests.

STANDARD FORMAT TESTS

Test 11: General Information

General Information (Rapid Reference 2.1) tests for an aspect of comprehension-knowledge (*Gc*), measuring the depth of one's general verbal knowledge. The General Information test contains two subtests: Where and What. In the former, the subject is asked, "Where would you find [an object]?" In the latter, the subject is asked, "What would you do with [an object]?" The initial items in each subtest draw from everyday objects, and the items become increasingly difficult as the objects become more obscure.

Administration
Be sure to review the exact pronunciation of the items before you begin testing. For some of the more difficult items, a pronunciation key is provided; you may also consult any standard dictionary. If the subject responds to a "What" question with a "Where" response, repeat the question using the complete sentence: "What would people usually do with [an object]?" Give this reminder only once during the administration of this subtest.

Item Scoring
A correct response is scored 1; an incorrect response is scored 0. Count unadministered items below the basal as correct.

CAUTION

Common Examiner Errors

Test 1: Verbal Comprehension
- Synonyms/Antonyms: Reading from the Test Record rather than from the Test Book (and therefore missing queries in the Test Book)
- Picture Vocabulary: Pointing to the wrong picture or part of picture

Test 2: Visual-Auditory Learning
- Not providing immediate feedback
- Correcting both parts of a compound word (words with suffix "-s" or "-ing") when only one part is incorrect
- Pushing the subject beyond his or her limits and administering the entire test when the subject is clearly frustrated and struggling

Test 3: Spatial Relations
- Scoring the first responses rather than the last responses given by the subject

Test 4: Sound Blending
- Not using the audio recording
- Not following general guidelines for audio-recorded tests

Test 5: Concept Formation
- Forgetting to follow pointing instructions for Introduction 2
- Not following the corrective feedback instructions
- Not using the same language as the subject when providing feedback (e.g., if the subject uses "pair" instead of "two," you should also use "pair")
- Acknowledging correct responses on Item 36 and beyond
- Not waiting for the subject to finish answering
- Failing to study and understand the queries presented in the Test Book

Test 6: Visual Matching
- Not following general guidelines for timed tests

Test 7: Numbers Reversed
- Reading from the Test Record rather than the Test Book
- Failing to leave a 1-s pause between numbers when administering items orally
- Not following the general guidelines for audio-recorded tests

Test 8: Incomplete Words
- Mispronouncing the phonemes when administering items orally
- Not following the general guidelines for audio-recorded tests

Test 9: Auditory Working Memory
- Giving partial credit for out-of-order responses (i.e., numbers before things)
- Not following the general guidelines for audio-recorded tests

Test 10: Visual-Auditory Learning–Delayed
- Administering the test when Visual Auditory Learning has not been administered in it's entirety
- Failing to give corrective feedback

Test 12: Retrieval Fluency
- Not giving credit for answers that may reflect a different cultural upbringing
- Not giving credit for different types of the same food, drink, or animal

Test 13: Picture Recognition
- Not scoring an item based on the last response given
- Giving the subject more or less than 5 s to view the stimulus page

Test 14: Auditory Attention
- Giving corrective feedback on items other than the training items
- Failing to retrain any missed training items
- Not turning the page quickly enough
- Replaying items from the audio recording
- Not following the general guidelines for audio-recorded tests

Test 15: Analysis-Synthesis
- Giving corrective feedback after Item 28
- Pointing to an item incorrectly
- Failing to read the paragraph below Sample Item E
- Not waiting until the subject has finished responding

Test 16: Decision Speed
- Not following the general guidelines for timed tests

Test 17: Memory for Words
- Not following the general guidelines for audio-recorded tests

(continued)

Test 18: Rapid Picture Naming
- Not turning the pages quickly enough

Test 19: Planning
- Not monitoring the subject carefully
- Incorrectly scoring items
- Not requiring the subject to mark an "X" where they begin

Test 20: Pair Cancellation
- Not following the general guidelines for timed tests

Test 11: General Information

Materials needed: Extended Battery Test Book and Test Record.

Starting point: Use "Suggested Starting Points" table in Test Book.

Basal (ceiling) criteria: Four lowest-numbered correct (four highest-numbered incorrect).

Tips:
- Make sure to pronounce each item correctly.
- Do not penalize for mispronunciations resulting from articulation errors, dialect variations, or regional speech patterns.
- Accept correct responses in other languages.

Test 12: Retrieval Fluency

Retrieval Fluency (Rapid Reference 2.2) measures an aspect of long-term retrieval (*Glr*), that is, fluency of retrieval from stored knowledge. The subject is asked to name as many examples as possible from a given category within a 1-min time span. The categories include things to eat or drink, first names of people, and animals.

Administration

Retrieval Fluency requires either a stopwatch, a digital watch, or a watch or clock with a second-hand. Administer Items 1 through 3 to all subjects. Each

≡ Rapid Reference 2.2

Test 12: Retrieval Fluency

Materials needed: Extended Battery Test Book and Test Record; stopwatch, digital watch, or watch/clock with second-hand.

Starting point: Item 1.

Basal (ceiling) criteria: None (none).

Tips:

- Administer all items to all subjects.
- Each item has a 1-min time limit.
- Use tally marks to record each correct response on the Test Record.
- Do not accept duplicate answers.
- Accept a correct response in another language as long as it does not duplicate an English response.
- Do not ask the subject to repeat.
- Do not penalize for mispronunciations resulting from articulation errors, dialect variations, or regional speech patterns.

item has a 1-min time limit. Do not count duplicate answers—for example, if the subject says "giraffe" three times, mark only one correct response. If you cannot remember whether the subject has duplicated a word, do not stop the subject or ask if the response was already named. Instead, give the response credit and balance the scores if you are unsure of another response. If the subject stops responding before the end of the time limit and says he or she has already given an answer, say, "Go ahead."

Item Scoring

Use tally marks on the lines provided in the Test Record to record the number of correct responses for each item. For Item 1, you may accept brand names of foods or drinks as correct (e.g., Coke, Spaghetti-O's). For either Item 1 or Item 3, you should accept different variations of the same type of food, drink, or animal. For example, if the subject says "grizzly bear, bear, black bear, polar bear," you should record four correct responses. For Item 2, you may also accept variations of the same name as correct (e.g., Bob, Bobby, Robert).

STANDARD FORMAT TESTS WITH SAMPLE/TRAINING ITEMS

Test 1: Verbal Comprehension

Verbal Comprehension (Rapid Reference 2.3) is made up of four subtests: Picture Vocabulary, Synonyms, Antonyms, and Verbal Analogies. Each subtest measures a different aspect of language development in spoken English. You must administer all four subtests in order to obtain derived scores for this test.

Picture Vocabulary measures aspects of lexical knowledge. This subtest requires the subject to identify pictures of familiar and unfamiliar objects. The beginning items require only a pointing response to pictures of common objects. The remaining items ask the subject to verbally identify the objects. The items become more difficult as the selected pictures appear less frequently in the environment or represent less familiar concepts.

The Synonyms and Antonyms subtests measure different aspects of vocabulary knowledge. In the Synonyms subtest, the person is given a word and

---

≡ Rapid Reference 2.3

Test 1: Verbal Comprehension

Materials needed: Standard Battery Test Book and Test Record.

Starting point: For 1A Picture Vocabulary, use "Suggested Starting Points" table in Test Book; for 1B Synonyms, 1C Antonyms, and 1D Verbal Analogies, administer sample items to all subjects, then use "Suggested Starting Points" table in Test Book.

Basal (ceiling) criteria: Three lowest-numbered correct (three highest-numbered incorrect).

Tips:

- Know the correct pronunciation for each test item.
- Accept responses that differ in tense or number.
- Do not accept responses that are different parts of speech.
- Request one-word responses unless otherwise noted.
- Do not penalize for mispronunciations resulting from articulation errors, dialect variations, or regional speech patterns.
- Accept correct responses in other languages.

is asked to provide a synonym. In the Antonyms subtest, the person is given a word and is asked to provide an antonym.

The Verbal Analogies subtest measures the subject's ability to reason using lexical knowledge. The subject hears three words of an analogy and is then asked to complete the analogy with an appropriate fourth word.

Administration

Know the correct pronunciation of all items before administering the test. On the Synonyms and Antonyms subtests, the correct pronunciation is in parentheses following the more difficult items; you may also refer to any standard dictionary. On Picture Vocabulary, point to the correct picture or the appropriate part of the picture as directed in the instructions for each item in the Test Book. Complete any Query listed in the Test Book.

Item Scoring

Score correct responses 1 and incorrect responses 0. Count all items below the basal as correct.

On Synonyms, Antonyms, and Verbal Analogies, responses are correct when they differ from the correct response only in verb tense or number (singular/plural), unless otherwise indicated by the scoring key. For example, on Item 7 of Verbal Analogies (*on* is to *start,* as *off* is to _____), the responses "stop," "stops," or "stopped" are all correct. A response is incorrect if the subject substitutes a different part of speech, such as a noun for a verb or an adjective, unless otherwise indicated by the scoring key. For example, on Item 10 of Antonyms (*life,* a noun), the responses "dead" (an adjective) and "dying" (a verb) are incorrect. Unless noted, only one-word responses are acceptable. If a person provides a two-word response, ask for a one-word answer. If a subject responds to an Antonym item by giving the stimulus word preceded by "non-" or "un-," ask for another answer unless otherwise indicated by the scoring key.

Test 3: Spatial Relations

Spatial Relations (Rapid Reference 2.4) is a test of visual-spatial thinking (*Gv*). This test requires the subject to identify two or three pieces that form a complete target shape. As the items progress and become more difficult, the drawings of the pieces are flipped, rotated, and become more similar in appearance.

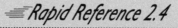

Rapid Reference 2.4

Test 3: Spatial Relations

Materials needed: Standard Battery Test Book and Test Record.

Starting point: Administer Introduction and sample items to all subjects, then begin with Item 1.

Basal (ceiling) criteria: None (determined by point totals at cutoffs).

Tips:

• Items may have multiple points for correct answers.

• If subject knows letter names, encourage subject to use letters to identify pieces, but allow pointing.

• If needed, use a paper or your hand to uncover one line at a time.

Administration

You may give corrective feedback as directed in the Test Book for the sample items only. If the presence of other items on the page confuses the subject, use your hand or a piece of paper to uncover one item at a time. Allow pointing responses, but if the subject knows letter names, encourage him or her to use letters for identifying the pieces. For items with 3 possible points, through Item 22, if the subject names only two pieces, say, "And what else?"

Item Scoring

Score 1 for each correctly identified piece, 0 for each incorrectly identified piece. (The total score for each item may be greater than 1.)

Test 6: Visual Matching

Visual Matching (Rapid Reference 2.5) is a test of processing speed (*Gs*) and, more specifically, perceptual speed. The task measures an aspect of cognitive efficiency—the speed at which an individual can make visual symbol discriminations. This test has two versions: Visual Matching 1 and Visual Matching 2. The first of these is designed for use with preschool children and individuals with developmental delays or reduced functioning. The task in Visual Matching 1 requires the subject to point to the two matching shapes in a row of four to five shapes. This section has a 2-min time limit and does not require the sub-

≣ Rapid Reference 2.5

Test 6: Visual Matching

Materials needed: Standard Battery Test Book and Test Record; stopwatch, digital watch, or watch/clock with a second-hand; pencil.

Starting point: Use "Suggested Starting Points" table in Test Book.

Basal (ceiling) criteria: None (none).

Tips:

• VM1 has a 2-min time limit; VM2 has a 3-min time limit.

• VM1: Cover extra lines as needed; VM2: Do not cover extra lines.

ject to write. The second version, Visual Matching 2, is designed for individuals who function at or above the level of an average 5-year-old. On this section, the subject is asked to locate and circle two identical numbers in a row of six within a 3-min time limit. The items become more difficult as they progress from single-digit numbers to triple-digit numbers.

Administration

Both versions of Visual Matching require a stopwatch, a digital watch, or a watch or clock with a second-hand. Visual Matching 2 also requires a pencil when prompted.

Visual Matching 1. This test is presented from the Test Book. If the subject is confused by more than one line per page, use a piece of paper or your hand to uncover one line at a time. This version has a 2-min time limit; if the subject does not use the full 2 min, record the exact finishing time in minutes and seconds on the Test Record. If you administer Visual Matching 1 first, and the subject has a score of 19 or more correct, administer Visual Matching 2 and use that score instead.

Visual Matching 2. This test is presented from the Test Record. Do not cover extra lines on the subject's page. This version has a 3-min time limit; if the subject does not use the full 3 min, record the exact finishing time in minutes and seconds on the Test Record. If you administer Visual Matching 2 first, and the subject has difficulty with the Practice Exercise, administer Visual Matching 1 and use that score instead.

Item Scoring

Score 1 point for each correctly identified pair. Use the scoring guide to score Visual Matching 2. On Visual Matching 2, score transposed numbers (e.g., 16 and 61) as incorrect. Do not count points for introductions, practice exercises, or sample items when calculating the number correct.

Test 13: Picture Recognition

Picture Recognition (Rapid Reference 2.6) measures visual memory of objects or pictures, an aspect of visual-spatial thinking (*Gv*). The subject's task is to recognize a subset of previously presented pictures within a field of distracting pictures. To eliminate verbal mediation as a memory strategy, varieties of the same type of object are used as the stimuli and distractors for each item (e.g., several different leaves or several different lamps). The difficulty of the items increases as the number of pictures in the stimulus set increases.

Administration

Each item consists of two pages of pictures: a stimulus page and a response page. Show the stimulus page for only 5 s. Request that the subject use letter names in his or her response; however, allow the subject to point if necessary.

Test 13: Picture Recognition

Materials needed: Extended Battery Test Book and Test Record.

Starting point: Administer sample items to all subjects, then begin with Item 1 for all subjects.

Basal (ceiling) criteria: None (determined by point totals at cutoffs).

Tips:

• Show stimulus for only 5 s.

• If subject knows letter names, encourage subject to use letters to identify pieces but allow pointing.

• If the subject gives more responses than necessary, score only the last ones given.

Item Scoring
Score 1 for each correctly recalled picture given in any order. If the subject gives more responses than required, score the last ones given (e.g., if four responses are given but only three are needed, base the score on the last three named).

Test 16: Decision Speed

Decision Speed (Rapid Reference 2.7) measures an aspect of Processing Speed (*Gs*)—the ability to make correct conceptual decisions quickly. In this test measuring the speed of processing simple concepts, the subject is presented with a row of objects and is asked to quickly locate the two pictures that are the most similar conceptually.

Administration
This test has a 3-min time limit and requires the use of the Subject Response Booklet and a pencil. Remind the subject not to erase (but to cross out) any pictures that were circled incorrectly. Although the subject may skip an item that seems difficult, he or she should proceed row by row. If the subject is confused by more than one line per page, you may use a piece of paper or your hand to

≡ Rapid Reference 2.7

Test 16: Decision Speed

Materials needed: Extended Battery Test Book, Subject Response Booklet, and Test Record; stopwatch, digital watch, or clock/watch with a second-hand; pencil.

Starting point: Administer sample items and practice exercises to all subjects, then begin with Item 1 for all subjects.

Basal (ceiling) criteria: None (none).

Tips:

• This test has a 3-min time limit.

• Cover rows of items if needed.

• If a subject cannot mark the similar items, have them point to the items while you mark them.

• Subject should cross out, not erase, any mistakes he or she makes.

uncover one line at a time. If the subject has difficulty with fine motor skills and cannot mark the items, ask him or her to point to the two related pictures, then mark the selected pictures yourself. If the subject finishes before the 3 min are up, record the exact finishing time in minutes and seconds on the Test Record.

Item Scoring

Both pictures must be marked to receive 1 point. For easier scoring, use the overlay scoring guide provided. If a subject marks two pictures that are loosely related (e.g., two living things or two things that may be in a house), score the response 0 because they are not the two pictures in the row that are considered the *most* alike.

Test 18: Rapid Picture Naming

Rapid Picture Naming (Rapid Reference 2.8) is a test of cognitive fluency that provides additional information about Processing Speed (*Gs*). This test measures the narrow ability of naming facility, or the speed of direct recall of information from acquired knowledge. The task requires the subject to quickly name a series of stimulus pictures.

≡ Rapid Reference 2.8

Test 18: Rapid Picture Naming

Materials needed: Extended Battery Test Book and Test Record; stopwatch, digital watch, or watch/clock with a second-hand.

Starting point: Administer sample items to all subjects, then begin with Item 1 for all subjects.

Basal (ceiling) criteria: None (none).

Tips:

• This test has a 2-min time limit.

• Turn page immediately after last item on each page.

• Accept synonyms, but not words that are only similar in meaning.

• Do not penalize mispronunciations resulting from articulation errors, dialect variations, or regional speech patterns.

• Accept correct responses in other languages.

Administration

This test has a 2-min time limit and requires the use of a stopwatch, a digital watch, or a watch or clock with a second-hand. Turn the page immediately after the subject has named the last item on the page. If the subject pauses for more than 2 s, say, "Try the next one." If the subject finishes before the end of 2 min, record the exact finishing time in minutes and seconds on the Test Record.

Item Scoring

Score correct responses 1, incorrect responses 0. If the subject uses a synonym, such as "kitty" or "kitten" for "cat," score the item correct. If the subject provides a word that is similar in meaning but is not a synonym, score the item incorrect (e.g., the subject uses "cup" for a picture of a glass).

Test 20: Pair Cancellation

Pair Cancellation (Rapid Reference 2.9) provides information about executive processing, attention/concentration, and Processing Speed (*Gs*) abilities. As an executive processing test, Pair Cancellation provides information about interference control. As a measure of attention/concentration, it provides in-

---

≡ Rapid Reference 2.9

Test 20: Pair Cancellation

Materials needed: Extended Battery Test Book, Subject Response Booklet, and Test Record; stopwatch, digital watch, or clock/watch with a second-hand; pencil.

Starting point: Administer Sample Item A and Practice Exercise to all subjects, then begin with Item I for all subjects.

Basal (ceiling) criteria: None (none).

Tips:

- This test has a 3-min time limit.
- Pair circled must contain a ball followed by a dog in the same row.
- Subject should cross out, not erase, any mistakes he or she makes.
- Do not provide the subject with a card or piece of paper to block out items during this test.

formation about sustained attention because the test requires the capacity to stay on task in a vigilant manner. Because the test is timed, Pair Cancellation also provides information about the subject's ability to perform a simple cognitive task under time pressure. The testing task requires the subject to find and mark a repeated pattern of objects throughout a page full of objects within a 3-min time period.

Administration

This test requires the use of the Subject Response Booklet, a pencil, and a stopwatch, digital watch, or a watch or clock with a second-hand. All subjects should complete Sample Item A and the Practice Exercise and then begin the test. Remind the subject not to erase (but to cross out) any pair that was circled incorrectly. Do not provide the subject with a card or paper to block the items on this test. If finishing time is not exactly 3 min, record exact finishing in minutes and seconds on the Test Record.

Item Scoring

Score 1 for each correct pair circled. If the subject scores 2 or fewer after the error correction procedure on the Practice Exercise, discontinue testing and record a 0. The pair circled must contain a ball followed by a dog in the same row. Both parts of the pair must be at least partially circled to receive credit. An overlay scoring guide is provided for easy scoring.

AUDIO RECORDING PRESENTATION TESTS

Test 4: Sound Blending

Sound Blending (Rapid Reference 2.10) is an auditory processing (*Ga*) test that measures skill in synthesizing language sounds. In this task, the subject listens to a series of syllables or phonemes and then is asked to blend the sounds into a word. The items become more difficult as the words are more complex and more fragmented.

Administration

Before beginning the test, locate Sample Item B on the audio recording and adjust the volume to a comfortable level. Present Sample Item A orally. If the subject does not understand the task, demonstrate further with the additional items provided in the "Error or No Response" box on the page in the Test

Rapid Reference 2.10

Test 4: Sound Blending

Materials needed: Standard Battery Test Book and Test Record; audio recording and audio equipment.

Starting point: Administer the sample items to all subjects, then begin with Item 1.

Basal (ceiling) criteria: None (six highest-numbered incorrect).

Tips:

• Use the audio recording to present Sample Item B and all test items.

• Word must be pronounced smoothly to receive credit.

• Do not repeat any items.

Book with the sample items. Present Sample Item B and all test items from the audio recording. Although the audio recording provides adequate time for most subjects to respond, examiners may pause or stop the recording if the subject needs more time. Because it is difficult to replicate the items orally, present this test using the audio recording; however, in rare cases, Items 1 through 16 may be presented orally. Attempt to say each item in the same manner that it is presented on the audio recording. Do not repeat any item during the test.

If the subject only pronounces the word phoneme by phoneme or syllable by syllable instead of saying it fluently (sounds not blended into a whole word), tell the subject, "Say the word smoothly." Give this reminder only once. Score the subject's last response. You may wish to record incorrect responses for later error analysis.

Item Scoring

Score correct responses 1, incorrect responses 0. If the subject pronounces the word in parts, as it is presented in the audio recording, score the item incorrect unless they self-correct.

Test 7: Numbers Reversed

Numbers Reversed (Rapid Reference 2.11) is a test of short-term memory (*Gsm*); it can also be classified as a measure of working memory or attentional

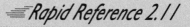

Rapid Reference 2.11

Test 7: Numbers Reversed

Materials needed: Standard Battery Test Book and Test Record; audio recording and audio equipment.

Starting point: Use "Suggested Starting Points" table in Test Book.

Basal (ceiling) criteria: Three lowest-numbered in group correct (three highest-numbered in group incorrect).

Tips:

• Use the audio recording to present Sample Item D and Items 11 through 30.

• Reminder to say numbers backward should be given only when indicated in Test Book.

• Do not repeat any items.

capacity. This task requires the subject to listen to a group of numbers and then repeat the numbers back in reverse order. The items grow more difficult as the strings of numbers become longer.

Administration

Before beginning the test, locate Sample Item D on the audio recording and adjust the volume to a comfortable level. Present Sample Items A through C and Items 1 through 10 orally; present Sample Item D and the remaining test items from the audio recording. Although the audio recording provides adequate time for most subjects to respond, examiners may pause or stop the recording if the subject needs more time. In rare cases, the items may be presented orally. Attempt to say each item in the same manner that it is presented on the audio recording—in an even voice at a rate of exactly one digit per second. Your voice should drop slightly on the last digit in each series to signal to the subject that the series has ended. Remind the subject to say the numbers in reverse only when indicated in the Test Book.

Item Scoring

Score each correct response 1, each incorrect response 0. Count all items below the basal as correct.

Rapid Reference 2.12

Test 8: Incomplete Words

Materials needed: Standard Battery Test Book and Test Record; audio recording and audio equipment.

Starting point: Use "Suggested Starting Points" table in Test Book.

Basal (ceiling) criteria: None (six highest-numbered incorrect).

Tips:

• Use the audio recording to present Sample Item E and all test items.

• Words must be pronounced as whole, unbroken words to receive credit.

• Do not repeat any items.

Test 8: Incomplete Words

Incomplete Words (Rapid Reference 2.12) provides information about auditory processing (*Ga*), including auditory analysis and auditory closure, aspects of phonemic awareness, and phonetic coding. In this task, the subject hears a word from the audio recording that is missing one or more phonemes. The subject is then asked to identify the complete word.

Administration

Before beginning the test, locate Sample Item E on the audio recording and adjust the volume to a comfortable level. Present Sample Items A through D orally. Present Sample Item E and the remaining items from the audio recording. Although the audio recording provides adequate time for most subjects to respond, examiners may pause or stop the audio recording if the subject needs more time. Because it is difficult to replicate the items orally, present this test using the audio recording; however, in rare cases, items 1 through 13 may be presented orally. Attempt to say each item in the same manner that it is presented on the audio recording. Do not repeat any items during the test.

If the subject only repeats the incomplete word just as it is pronounced on the audio recording, say, "Tell me the whole word that he is trying to say." Give this reminder only once during administration of this test. Score the subject's last response. You may wish to record incorrect responses for later error analysis.

Item Scoring

Score correct responses 1, incorrect responses 0. Although the test instructions imply that only single-word answers are correct, the scoring key includes several acceptable two- and three-word answers.

Test 9: Auditory Working Memory

Auditory Working Memory (Rapid Reference 2.13) measures short-term memory span; it can also be classified as a measure of working memory or divided attention. The task requires the ability to hold information in immediate awareness, divide the information into two groups, and shift attentional resources to the two new-ordered sequences. This test asks the subject to listen to a series that contains both digits and words, such as "dog, 1, shoe, 8, 2, apple." The subject then attempts to reorder the information, repeating first the objects in sequential order, and then the digits in sequential order.

Administration

Before beginning the test, locate the correct starting item on the audio recording and adjust the volume to a comfortable level. Present Sample Item A orally. Present all other sample items and test items from the audio recording. Although the audio recording provides adequate time for most subjects to respond, you may pause or stop the recording if a subject needs more time. In

---

≡ Rapid Reference 2.13

Test 9: Auditory Working Memory

Materials needed: Standard Battery Test Book and Test Record; audio recording and audio equipment.

Starting point: Administer Sample Item A to all subjects, then use "Suggested Starting Points" table in Test Book.

Basal (ceiling) criteria: Three lowest-numbered in group correct (three highest-numbered in group incorrect).

Tips:
- Words must be attempted before digits to receive any points.
- Accept words that sound similar to, or rhyme with, the target words.

rare cases, the items may be presented orally. Attempt to say each item in the same manner that it is presented on the audio recording—in an even voice at a rate of exactly one word or digit per second. Your voice should drop slightly at the end of the series to signal the subject that the series has ended.

Item Scoring

Score an item 2 if the subject states the objects in the correct order, followed by the digits in the correct order. Score an item 1 if the subject states the objects or the digits in the correct order; the person must attempt to repeat the words *before* the digits. Score an item 0 if the subject states neither the objects nor the digits in the correct order or responds with the digits first. Responses are scored as correct if they sound very similar to (e.g., "cap" for "cat") or if they rhyme with (e.g., "neat" for "meat") a test word. Count all items below the basal as correct.

Test 14: Auditory Attention

Auditory Attention (Rapid Reference 2.14) measures an aspect of speech-sound discrimination—the ability to overcome the effects of auditory distortion or masking in understanding oral language. This is a test of narrow auditory processing (*Ga*) ability requiring selective attention. The subject listens to a word while looking at four pictures and is asked to point to the correct picture for the word. Difficulty increases as the added background

≡ Rapid Reference 2.14

Test 14: Auditory Attention

Materials needed: Extended Battery Test Book and Test Record; audio recording and audio equipment.

Starting point: Administer Training Items and Sample Items, then begin with Item 1 for all subjects.

Basal (ceiling) criteria: None (six highest-numbered incorrect).

Tips:
- All test items must be presented from the audio recording.
- Do not replay any items or stop the recording during administration.

noise becomes louder and the sound discriminations become more difficult.

Administration

Before beginning the test, locate Item 1 on the audio recording and adjust the volume to a comfortable level. Present the training items orally. If the subject does not respond or responds incorrectly to a training item, point to the correct picture, say the picture's name, and, if necessary, explain what the picture represents. After presenting the last training item, return to any items that were missed and readminister those items.

Administer Sample Items A through C orally. Present all test items from the audio recording. Because of the gradually increasing background noise, this test cannot be validly administered without the audio recording. Do not replay an item or pause or stop the audio recording even if the subject responds slowly. Turn the page quickly after the last item on each page has been presented by the audio recording.

Item Scoring

Score correct responses 1, incorrect responses 0. Do not count points for training items or sample items when calculating the number correct.

Test 17: Memory for Words

Memory for Words (Rapid Reference 2.15) measures auditory short-term memory (*Gsm*). This test asks the subject to repeat lists of unrelated words in the correct sequence.

Administration

Before beginning the test, locate the correct starting item on the audio recording and adjust the volume to a comfortable level. Present Sample Items A and B orally. If the subject does not understand the task, demonstrate further with additional pairs of words that are provided in the "Error or No Response" box on the page in the Test Book with the sample items. Present all test items from the audio recording. Although the audio recording provides adequate time for most subjects to respond, you may pause or stop the recording if he or she needs more time. In rare cases, the items may be presented orally. Attempt to say each item in the same manner that it is presented on the audio recording—

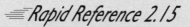

Rapid Reference 2.15

Test 17: Memory for Words

Materials needed: Extended Battery Test Book and Test Record; audio recording and audio equipment.

Starting point: Administer Sample Items A and B to all subjects, then use "Suggested Starting Points" table in Test Book.

Basal (ceiling) criteria: Three lowest-numbered in group correct (three highest-numbered in group incorrect).

Tips:

• Words must be in exact order to receive credit.

• Accept words that sound similar to or rhyme with target words.

in an even voice at a rate of exactly one word per second. The examiner's voice should drop slightly on the last word in each series to signal the subject that the series has ended.

Item Scoring

Score correct responses 1, incorrect responses 0. Count items below the basal as correct. The subject must repeat the words in the exact order that they were presented to receive credit for an item. Responses are correct if they sound very similar to (e.g., "son" for "some") or if they rhyme with (e.g., "bat" for "that") a test word.

CONTROLLED LEARNING TESTS

Test 2: Visual-Auditory Learning

Visual-Auditory Learning (Rapid Reference 2.16) is a test of long-term retrieval (*Glr*) that requires the subject to learn, store, and retrieve a series of visual-auditory associations. The subject is asked to learn and recall a series of rebuses (pictographic representations of words) that, eventually, are combined into phrases, and then sentences of increasing length and complexity.

Administration

Because Visual-Auditory Learning is a controlled learning task, all subjects must have an identical opportunity to learn. Administer this test without in-

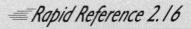

Rapid Reference 2.16

Test 2: Visual-Auditory Learning

Materials needed: Standard Battery Test Book and Test Record.
Starting point: Administer Introduction 1 and Test Story 1 to all subjects.
Basal (ceiling) criteria: None (determined by error totals at cutoffs).
Tips:

- This test requires exact administration.
- Missed words, extra words, and synonyms are considered errors.
- Allow 5 s for subject to respond before pointing to the symbol and providing the word.
- When a subject makes a mistake, immediately point to the symbol and provide the word.
- Do not allow the subject to practice or review symbols.
- If you will administer Visual-Auditory Learning–Delayed, do not tell the subject that he or she will need to recall the symbols/words later.
- Score is the number of errors.

terruptions. Before administering the test, record the date and time of administration on the Test Record. This information is important if Visual-Auditory Learning–Delayed will be administered.

Give immediate, corrective feedback when a subject makes an error but do not acknowledge correct responses. If the subject makes an error or pauses for longer than 5 s, point to the symbol, say its name, and then point to the next symbol. During the test, it may be helpful if you keep your nondominant hand near the top of the easel to provide feedback quickly and easily with a small movement. Do not discuss the symbols or help the subject to form associations between the symbols and the words they represent.

When new symbols are introduced, the task requires the subject to verbalize the symbol name. You should not repeat the symbol name and the subject should respond to a symbol only once each time it is presented. To ensure that the subject does not have additional time to study the symbols on the introduction pages, turn the page as soon as the subject has named the last symbol. On the first story, point word-by-word until the subject understands that he or she is supposed to read the symbols. If necessary, you may continue pointing throughout the test. If the presence of several lines on the page confuses the subject, use your hand or a piece of paper to uncover one line at a time.

The arrows on the examiner's side of the Test Book (on Introduction 7) indicate that you should slide a finger from the new symbol (i.e., "ing" and "s") to the other two symbols (i.e., "riding" and "trees") and across them. This movement reinforces the idea that two symbols (morphemes) will blend together to form a whole word.

If administering Visual-Auditory Learning–Delayed, do not tell the subject during or after the administration of Visual-Auditory Learning that he or she is going to be asked at a later time to recall or relearn the symbols. If Visual-Auditory Learning–Delayed will be administered within the same testing session, administer *all* of Visual-Auditory Learning near the beginning of the testing session to allow for the greatest length of time between the tests.

Item Scoring

Circle each word that the subject misses or that you have to tell to the subject after a 5-s pause. If the subject gives a synonym for a word, such as "small" for "little," count the response as an error. On words with two syllables, such as "ride . . . ing," each symbol is a possible error. If the subject responds incorrectly to the first symbol, correct the error without naming the second symbol. If the subject skips a word, point to the skipped word and say, "What is this?" If the subject inserts a word, record the word on the Test Record, circle it, and count it as an error. Count the total number of errors for determining the test cutoff points.

Test 5: Concept Formation

Concept Formation (Rapid Reference 2.17) is a test of fluid reasoning (Gf) that involves categorical reasoning based on principles of inductive logic. This test also measures an aspect of executive processing—flexibility in thinking when required to shift one's mental set frequently. Unlike some concept formation tasks that require a subject to remember what has happened over a series of items, this test does not include a memory component. The Concept Formation task requires the subject to examine a stimulus set and then formulate a rule that applies to the item.

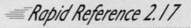

Test 5: Concept Formation

Materials needed: Standard Battery Test Book and Test Record.
Starting point: Use "Suggested Starting Points" table in Test Book.
Basal (ceiling) criteria: None (determined by point totals at cutoffs).
Tips:
• This test requires exact administration.
• Accept synonyms as correct.
• Acknowledge correct responses and provide corrective feedback through Item 35.
• Items 27 through 40 have a 1-min time limit.

Administration

This test is a controlled learning task that requires exact administration and uninterrupted presentation. Pay close attention to the pointing instructions in Introduction 1, Items 1 through 5, and Introduction 2. Do not provide the subject with any additional explanation. If the presence of rows of geometric shapes on the page confuses the subject, use your hand or a piece of paper to uncover one line at a time.

On Sample Item C through Item 35, acknowledge correct responses or give immediate, corrective feedback for incorrect responses. You should vary the acknowledgment of correct responses. For example, give a nod of the head and/or comments such as "good," "right," or "that's correct." Do not allow signs of acknowledgment to become an automatic reaction to all responses, including incorrect ones—this will confuse the subject and destroy the learning nature of the task. When giving feedback or making corrections using the "Error or No Response" box, use the same word(s) that the subject used. Do not acknowledge correct or incorrect responses on Items 36 through 40.

There is a 1-min time limit per item for Items 27 through 40. If the subject's time exceeds 1 min, follow the directions in the "Error or Over 1 Minute" boxes in the Test Book.

Item Scoring

Score correct responses 1, incorrect responses 0. If the subject began with Introduction 2 and received a score of 1 or 0 correct on Items 6 through 11, pre-

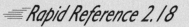

Rapid Reference 2.18

Test 10: Visual-Auditory Learning–Delayed

Materials needed: Standard Battery Test Book and Test Record.
Starting point: Line 1.
Basal (ceiling) criteria: None (none).
Tips:

- Administer this test only if you have administered Visual-Auditory Learning in its entirety.
- This test requires exact administration.
- Missed words, extra words, and synonyms are considered errors.
- Allow 5 s for subject to respond before pointing to the symbol and providing the word.
- When a subject makes a mistake, immediately point to the symbol and provide the word.
- Score is the number of errors.

sent Introduction 1 and Items 1 through 5, and then discontinue testing (base the subject's score on Items 1 through 11). Score an item correct if the subject provides a synonym or word that is similar in meaning to the word provided in the scoring key.

Test 10: Visual-Auditory Learning–Delayed

This test can be used to provide additional information about long-term retrieval (*Glr*) abilities, specifically aspects of associative and meaningful memory. Visual-Auditory Learning–Delayed (Rapid Reference 2.18) is presented 30 min to 8 days after Visual-Auditory Learning; it is a memory exercise that requires the subject to recall the symbol/word relationships learned in Visual-Auditory Learning.

Administration

Administer Visual-Auditory Learning–Delayed only if you have administered *all* of Visual-Auditory Learning (from 30 min to 8 days previously). Because this test is a controlled learning task, all subjects must have an identical opportunity to learn. Do not discuss symbols or help the subject to form associations between the symbols and the words they represent. Give immediate, corrective feedback when a subject makes an error, but do not acknowledge correct responses. If a subject makes an error or pauses for longer than 5 s, point to the symbol, say its name, and then point to the next symbol. If the presence of several lines on the page confuses the subject, use a hand or piece of paper to uncover one line at a time.

Item Scoring

Circle each word that the subject misses or that you have to tell the subject after a 5-s pause. Do not accept synonyms as correct. On words with two symbols, such as "ride . . . ing," each symbol is a possible error. If the subject responds incorrectly to the first symbol, correct the error without naming the second symbol. Count the total number of errors for determining the test cutoff points.

Test 15: Analysis-Synthesis

Analysis-Synthesis (Rapid Reference 2.19) is a test of fluid reasoning (*Gf*) that measures general sequential (deductive) reasoning. The test is a controlled learning task and is designed to measure the ability to reason and draw conclusions from given conditions. The subject is given instructions on how to perform an increasingly complex procedure that requires him or her to examine and solve a series of puzzles.

Administration

Because Analysis-Synthesis is a controlled learning test, it requires exact administration. Begin the test with the Color Pretest for all subjects. If the subject cannot be trained on the Color Pretest, check "Untrainable" on the Test Record and discontinue testing.

Pay particular attention to the queries on the first few sample items. Also pay particular attention to the pointing instructions for all items, including the three introductions. Do not provide the subject with any additional explanation. If the presence of several puzzles on the page confuses the subject, use your hand or a piece of paper to uncover one item at a time.

On Sample Item A through Item 28, acknowledge correct responses or give immediate, corrective feedback for incorrect responses following the "Error or No Response" boxes in the Test Book. You should vary the acknowledg-

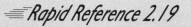

Rapid Reference 2.19

Test 15: Analysis-Synthesis

Materials needed: Extended Battery Test Book and Test Record.
Starting point: Administer the Color Pretest, then administer Introduction I and sample items to all subjects.
Basal (ceiling) criteria: None (determined by point totals at cutoffs).
Tips:

- This test requires exact administration.
- Provide corrective feedback for errors through Item 28.
- Acknowledge correct responses through Item 28.
- Items 26 through 35 each have a 1-min time limit.

ment of correct responses. For example, give a nod of the head and/or provide comments such as "good," "right," or "that's correct." Do not allow signs of acknowledgment to become an automatic reaction to all responses, including incorrect ones—this will confuse the subject and destroy the learning nature of the task. Do not acknowledge correct or incorrect responses on Items 29 to 35.

There is a 1-min time limit per item for Items 26 through 35. If the subject's time exceeds 1 min, follow the directions in the "Error or Over 1 Minute" boxes in the Test Book.

Item Scoring

Score correct responses 1 and incorrect responses 0. Do not assign a score for the test if the "Untrainable" box was checked on the Test Record.

TESTS WITH SPECIAL SCORING PROCEDURES

Test 19: Planning

Planning (Rapid Reference 2.20) is a test of executive processing that measures the mental control process involved in determining, selecting, and applying solutions to problems using forethought. This test is a complex task that draws on Fluid Reasoning (*Gf*) and Visual-Spatial Thinking (*Gv*) abilities, and re-

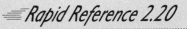

Rapid Reference 2.20

Test 19: Planning

Materials needed: Extended Battery Test Book, Subject Response Booklet, and Test Record; pencil with eraser.

Starting point: Administer Sample Items A through C to all subjects, then use "Suggested Starting Points" table in Test Book.

Basal (ceiling) criteria: None (none).

Tips:

- Follow Continuation Instructions to determine when to discontinue testing.
- Monitor the subject closely for retracing or lifting pencil.
- Erasing is not allowed on any test item.
- Score is the number of errors.

quires the subject to trace a pattern without removing his or her pencil from the paper or retracing any lines. As the items progress, the patterns become more complex.

Administration

This test requires the Subject Response Booklet and a pencil. Follow the Continuation Instructions to determine when to discontinue testing. Watch the subject carefully on each item to monitor his or her errors. If the subject retraces a line or attempts to erase, stop the subject, remind him or her not to retrace or erase, then proceed to the next item. If the subject lifts the pencil, remind him or her not to lift the pencil and then allow the subject to continue from exactly where he or she left off. Erasing lines is permitted only on the sample items. Although the subject may skip an item that seems difficult, he or she should proceed item by item.

Item Scoring

In this test, you must count the number of errors to calculate a score. On the examiner's pages in the Test Book, each item is divided into segments and each segment is a potential error. The segments are defined by color and separated by space. Score each retraced and/or uncompleted segment as an error. As the subject completes a page, score the items immediately in order to follow the continuation instructions.

✍ TEST YOURSELF ✍

1. The first page after the tab in each test provides general information and instructions specific to that test. True or False?

2. When administering a test, always use the exact wording and instructions presented in the Test Book. True or False?

3. The best seating arrangement is one in which you and the subject sit directly across a table from each other. True or False?

4. The best practice is to test by complete pages when stimulus material appears on the subject's side of the Test Book. True or False?

5. Which of the following is not an acceptable accommodation?

   (a) frequent breaks

   (b) additional testing time on non-timed tests

   (c) use of a calculator

   (d) special furniture

6. Modifications to the standardized testing procedure can fundamentally alter the results and validity of the test results. True or False?

7. Which of the following tests does not require use of the standardized audio recording?

   (a) Verbal Comprehension

   (b) Sound Blending

   (c) Auditory Working Memory

   (d) Numbers Reversed

8. Which of the following tests does not require use of a stopwatch, digital watch, or a watch or clock with a second-hand?

   (a) Visual Matching

   (b) Retrieval Fluency

   (c) Rapid Picture Naming

   (d) Auditory Attention

9. It takes approximately 45 to 50 min to administer the tests in the Standard Battery and 1.5 to 1.75 hr to administer the tests in the complete Battery. True or False?

10. The correct and incorrect keys in the Test Book do not include all possible responses. True or False?

Answers: 1. True; 2. True; 3. False; 4. True; 5. c; 6. True; 7. a; 8. d; 9. True; 10. True

Three

HOW TO SCORE THE WJ III COG

The WJ III COG cannot be scored without the use of the WJ III Compuscore and Profiles Program (WJ III CPP; Schrank & Woodcock, 2001). This scoring software is included with every WJ III COG package. Your job as an examiner is to correctly interpret and record the subject's answers for use in the software entry screens. Once you have determined the raw scores, the WJ III CPP calculates derived scores and discrepancies and allows you to choose from several scoring and interpretive options.

This chapter includes the essential criteria needed to calculate item scores for each test, including a section emphasizing the three tests requiring special scoring procedures. A brief description of the reporting options available with the WJ III CPP is also presented in this chapter. Finally, the chapter outlines the step-by-step procedures for scoring each WJ III COG test.

ITEM SCORING

Two sets of scores are calculated when you administer the WJ III COG. First, you will determine individual item scores for each item administered. Because basal and ceiling levels are determined by an examinee's pattern of correct and incorrect responses, individual items are scored *during* test administration. Second, you will calculate the total item score, or raw score, following completion of the testing session. Generally, the raw score is determined by adding the number of correctly completed items to the number of test items below the basal. However, for some tests such as Test 2: Visual Auditory Learning, Test 10: Visual-Auditory Learning–Delayed, and Test 19: Planning, the raw score is determined by summing the number of errors.

The majority of items comprising the WJ III COG tests are scored by recording a 1 (correct) or 0 (incorrect) in the appropriate space on the Test Record. Spaces corresponding with items not administered are left blank. Items not administered generally include items either below the basal or above the ceiling as well as items that are not in the assigned block of administered items. Rapid Reference 3.1 lists useful notations that you can use when recording item responses.

TESTS REQUIRING SPECIAL SCORING PROCEDURES

=== *Rapid Reference 3.1*

Notations for Recording Responses

I	Correct response*
0	Incorrect, or no response*
Q	Indicates a query
DK	Indicates the response of "Don't Know"
NR	Indicates "No Response"
SC	Indicates a self-correction

*Except for Tests 2, 10, and 19.
Source: Adapted from *WJ III Tests of Cognitive Abilities Examiner's Manual*, p. 35, Riverside Publishing 2001.

Of the 20 tests in the WJ III COG, three tests have special scoring procedures: Test 2: Visual-Auditory Learning, Test 10: Visual-Auditory Learning–Delayed, and Test 19: Planning. While raw scores on most tests are computed by counting the number of correct responses, the raw scores for Tests 2, 10, and 19 are derived by counting the total number of errors. Details for these three tests are summarized in the following sections; while studying them you should have a copy of the WJ III COG Test Record in hand. For additional information, consult the WJ III COG *Examiner's Manual* (Mather & Woodcock, 2001).

Test 2: Visual Auditory Learning

The score for Visual-Auditory Learning is based on the total number of errors. Omitted words, inserted words, synonyms (e.g., "little" for "small"), and non-responses are scored as errors. A nonresponse occurs when the examinee fails to provide a response within 5 seconds. In such cases, the correct response is provided by the examiner and the symbol is considered an error. For words with two symbols (e.g., "ride . . . ing"), each symbol is considered separately in scoring. Thus, if *one* part of a two-symbol word is incorrect and the other cor-

DON'T FORGET

- Whenever possible, record incorrect responses in the Test Record. A subsequent analysis of these responses will be helpful in developing clinical inferences and recommendations.
- Correct and incorrect answer keys are guides; you may have to use judgment in determining the correctness of a response.
- Score the last answer given.
- Use your professional judgment in answering and asking questions of the subject.

rect, only one symbol is counted as an error. If *both* parts of a two-symbol word are incorrect (e.g., the examinee does not provide a response within 5 s), two errors are recorded. Errors are counted throughout the entire administration and are periodically recorded in cutoff boxes that appear on the Test Record. Once errors are calculated, the number of errors and the letter corresponding to the Test Stories administered are recorded in the "Software Score Entry" box appearing on the Test Record. If you plan to administer Test 10: Visual-Auditory Learning–Delayed, all of Test 2: Visual-Auditory Learning must be administered, regardless of the number of errors. Additionally, if the delayed portion of this test is to be administered, the "Date" and "Time" spaces on the Test Record must be completed at the start of testing.

Test 10: Visual-Auditory Learning–Delayed

This test is scored in the same manner as Visual-Auditory Learning. Thus, each incorrectly read symbol is scored 1. Similarly, the definition of what constitutes an error is identical for both tests; omissions, insertions, synonyms, and non-responses are all considered errors. However, unlike Visual-Auditory Learning, there are no cutoff boxes in which to record errors. Rather, the total number of errors is summed and recorded in the "Number of Errors" box on the Test Record. Finally, the administration date and time of Visual-Auditory Learning–Delayed is recorded in the "Date" and "Time" spaces on the Test Record.

Test 19: Planning

Like Visual-Auditory Learning and Visual-Auditory Learning–Delayed, the raw score for Test 19: Planning is based on the total number of errors. Each incorrect response is scored as 1. Because the items on the Planning test are composed of line segments, each segment within an item is a potential error. Segments are delineated by color and separated by space on the examiner's pages in the Test Book. Retraced or uncompleted segments are considered errors. The total number of errors for each item is recorded in the space provided to the left of the item in the Test Record. Additionally, the total number of errors for each page of items is summed and recorded in the corresponding cutoff box on the Test Record. Finally, the number of errors for the specific block of items administered is recorded in the "Software Score Entry" box on the Test Record. If a particular block of items was not administered, an "X" is placed in the "Software Score Entry" box for those items. In addition to software score entry instructions, information regarding hand scoring is available in the "Hand Scoring Only" box on the Test Record. It is important to note that although summing the total number of errors on the Planning test is straightforward, identifying errors during testing requires you to watch the examinee closely. For instance, although retraced segments may be apparent by visual inspection of the examinee's response booklet, this is not always the case; thus, it is important that you watch the examinee physically trace the line segments to ensure that you identify any errors as they occur. Additionally, you should note the examinee's starting point for each item.

CAUTION

Common Errors in Obtaining Raw Scores

- Forgetting to award credit for all items below the basal
- Including sample items in the computation of the raw score
- Committing simple addition errors
- Transposing numbers
- Neglecting to enter the raw scores for each subtest within a test (e.g., Test 2: Verbal Comprehension and Test 11: General Information), for each item (e.g., Test 12: Retrieval Fluency), or for each set of items (e.g., Test 19: Planning)
- Neglecting to enter an "X" for each set of items not administered on Test 19: Planning
- Transferring the raw score incorrectly to the computer program or scoring table

STEP-BY-STEP: HOW TO SCORE THE WJ III COG

Step 1: Obtaining Raw Scores

With the exception of three tests (Test 2: Visual-Auditory Learning, Test 10: Visual-Auditory Learning–Delayed, and Test 19: Planning), the computation of raw scores follows the same procedure. That is, the raw score is obtained by totaling the item scores for the correct responses in addition to scores for every item in the test below the basal. Although scores for sample or practice items are recorded in the Test Record, they should not be included when calculating raw scores. Sample or practice items appear in shaded panels to distinguish them from the actual test items.

The computed raw score is recorded in the shaded "Number Correct" box in each test section of the Test Record. The computation of raw scores can be completed prior to administering the next test or may be completed as the examinee is working on subsequent tests.

The three tests that are exceptions to the basic procedure were discussed in detail earlier in the "Tests Requiring Special Scoring Procedures" section. For Test 2: Visual-Auditory Learning and Test 10: Visual-Auditory Learning–Delayed, the raw score is based on the number of incorrect responses. Similarly, for Test 19: Planning, the raw score is based on the errors made on each of the pages administered.

Step 2: Obtaining Estimated Age and Grade Equivalent Scores (Optional)

If needed, you may manually obtain estimates of the age and grade equivalents for each test by using the scoring tables in the Test Record. With the exception of Test 10: Visual-Auditory Learning–Delayed, each test in the Test Record contains scoring tables. This optional procedure is available if you need to obtain immediate developmental information. By utilizing the information provided in each test's scoring table, you can receive immediate feedback during the testing session regarding the examinee's estimated level of performance. Such feedback may serve to refine the selection of starting points in later tests or suggest the need for further testing. The estimated scores obtained from these tables may differ slightly (less than 1 SEM) from

Test 4 Sound Blending
Scoring Table
Encircle row for the Number Correct.

Number Correct	Age Equivalents	Grade Equivalents
0	<2-9	<K.0
1	2-11	<K.0
2	3-3	<K.0
3	3-5	<K.0
4	3-8	<K.0
5	3-10	<K.0
6	4-1	<K.0
7	4-3	<K.0
8	4-6	<K.0
9	4-10	<K.0
10	5-1	K.1
11	5-5	K.2
12	5-10	K.4
13	6-3	K.7
14	6-9	1.0
15	7-4	1.4
16	8-0	1.9
17	8-9	2.8
18	9-8	4.0
19	10-8	5.4
20	11-11	6.8
21	13-4	8.4
22	15-1	9.9
23	17-5	11.5
24	21	12.9
25	>26	13.0
26	>26	13.9
>26	>26	>18.0

Note: Age equivalents and grade equivalents are estimates of the precise valves provided by the software scoring program.

Figure 3.1 Obtaining the Estimated Age and Grade Equivalents Corresponding with 24 Correct on Test 4: Sound Blending

Source: Adapted from *WJ III Tests of Cognitive Abilities* Test Record, p. 5, Riverside Publishing 2001.

the actual age equivalent (AE) and grade equivalent (GE) scores reported by the WJ III CPP.

Following test scoring, you can locate the number corresponding to the raw score in the first column of the test's scoring table on the Test Record and circle the entire row. The circled row provides the raw score (Raw), estimated AE, and estimated GE. Figure 3.1 illustrates the completion of this step for an eighth-grade girl who obtained a raw score of 24 on Test 4: Sound Blending.

Step 3: Using the WJ III Compuscore and Profiles Program

The remainder of the scoring procedure is completed using the WJ III Compuscore and Profiles Program (WJ III CPP). To obtain derived scores, enter the examinee identification information, the raw score for each test administered, and the information from the "Test Session Observations Checklist" on the Test Record.

From the "Reports" menu, you may select a Score Report, a Summary and Score Report, an Age/Grade Profile, a Standard Score/Percentile Rank (SS/PR) Profile, or any combination of these reports. You will then need to select a normative group—including age norms, grade norms, and 2- and 4-year college norms—for comparative purposes.

If you have administered the appropriate tests, and you want to include the GIA or BIA scores in the report, you should check "Include GIA/BIA Scores." You can also select any discrepancy procedures you wish to have calculated. Always double-check to make sure the desired selections have been made.

You should use the "Options" menu if you want to include any additional scores in the report, such as a z-score for Test 10: Visual-Auditory Learning–Delayed. Make sure you have your discrepancy cutoffs and SS confidence bands at the desired settings. Note that you may include either the individual's raw score or W-score on the table of scores.

Any options selected may be saved to ensure that future reports will use those same options. The examinee data, narrative report, and table of scores also may be saved. The profiles (Age/Grade, SS/PR) can be printed, but not saved or exported. Only the narrative report and table of scores can be exported to a word processing program.

REMINDERS FOR SCORING EACH TEST

Test 1: Verbal Comprehension

Range: A, 0–23; B, 0–15; C, 0–18; D, 0–15
Scoring Reminders:

- All four subtests must be administered to obtain derived scores.
- Score correct responses 1, incorrect responses 0.
- 1B Synonyms, 1C Antonyms, and 1D Verbal Analogies require administration of sample items. For these sections, a response is scored 1 if it

DON'T FORGET

Computer-Generated Scores

The software program that comes with the WJ III is used to generate all derived scores; manually, only estimated age and grade equivalents for the individual tests can be obtained. Cluster scores, based on the tests administered, are available only with the WJ III CPP.

Test-Session Validity

There are two questions on the front page of each Test Record that should be answered: "Do these test results provide a fair representation of the subject's present functioning?" and "Were any modifications made to the standardized test procedures during this administration?"

If you have some reason for questioning the test results, mark "Yes" to the first question and provide an explanation in the space provided. Possible reasons for questioning validity include (a) hearing or vision difficulties, (b) behavioral or attentional difficulties that interfere with the examinee's ability to concentrate, and (c) certain background variables (e.g., limited English proficiency). Record any unusual test behaviors or answers that arise during testing because qualitative information of this nature can become significant during the analysis of test results.

If you did not follow the standardized test procedures exactly as prescribed in the examiner's manuals or in this book, or if you did not use the exact wording provided on the examiner's side of the easel, you must check "Yes" in response to the second question and provide a description of the modifications that were made. Be sure to transfer this information to the WJ III CPP. A "Yes" response to either question may call into question the validity of the test results.

differs from the correct answer in verb tense or number; a response is incorrect if it is a different part of speech from the correct answer.

- Enter number of items answered correctly plus one point for each item below the basal in the "Number Correct" box.

Test 2: Visual-Auditory Learning

Range: A, 0–6; B, 0–12; C, 0–40; D, 0–81; E, 0–109
Scoring Reminders:

- All of Test 2: Visual-Auditory Learning must be administered if Test 10: Visual-Auditory Learning–Delayed is to be administered, regardless of the number of errors.

- Be sure to record the date and time of the test protocol before administering the test. This information is necessary when entering test data into the WJ III CPP.
- Circle each word the subject misses or is told after a 5-s pause. The number of errors will be used to score this test.
- Omitted words and inserted words are scored as an error.
- For words with two symbols (e.g., "ride . . . ing"), each symbol is considered separately in scoring. If one part of a two-symbol word is incorrect, score only the incorrect part as an error.
- If an examinee fails to provide a response within 5 s, point to the symbol, say the word, and score the nonresponse as an error.
- Record the total number of errors at each cutoff point in the box provided on the test protocol.
- To ensure accuracy when entering scores into the software program, enter the number of errors and the letter corresponding to the Test Stories administered in the "Software Score Entry" box on the test protocol.

Test 3: Spatial Relations

Range: A, 0–11; B, 0–27; C, 0–57; D, 0–81
Scoring Reminders:

- Score each correctly identified piece of an item 1.
- Sum the correctly identified pieces for each item (0 to 2 for 2-point items; 0 to 3 for 3-point items), and record this number to the left of the item on the test protocol page.
- Record the total number of points for a set of items in the corresponding cutoff box provided on the test protocol.
- To ensure accuracy when entering scores into the software program, record the total number of points and the letter corresponding to the block of items administered in the "Software Score Entry" box on the test protocol.

Test 4: Sound Blending

Range: 0–33
Scoring Reminders:

- Score correct responses 1, incorrect responses 0.
- Items that are pronounced in parts (as they are on the audiocassette) are considered errors and scored 0.
- Sum the number of points for all items and record the total in the "Number Correct" box on the test protocol.

Test 5: Concept Formation

Range: A, 0–5; B, 0–11; C, 0–20; D, 0–29; E, 0–40
Scoring Reminders:

- Score correct responses 1, incorrect responses 0.
- If an examinee provides a synonym for a word provided in the scoring key (e.g., "small" for "little"), the item is considered correct and scored 1.
- If the first five items were not administered, consider all five items correct when calculating the total score.
- Record the total number of points for a set of items in the corresponding cutoff box provided on the test protocol.
- To ensure accuracy when entering scores into the software program, record the total number correct and the letter corresponding to the block of items administered in the "Software Score Entry" box on the test protocol.

Test 6: Visual Matching

Range: Version 1, 0–26; Version 2, 0–60
Scoring Reminders:

- Score 1 for each correctly identified pair.
- Transposed numbers (e.g., 17 and 71) on Visual Matching 2 are considered errors.

- To facilitate scoring on Visual Matching 2, use the scoring template provided.
- Introductions, practice exercises, and sample items are not counted as points when calculating the total number correct.
- Record the completion time (in minutes and seconds) in the "Time" section on the test protocol. The time limit is 2 min for Visual Matching 1 and 3 min for Visual Matching 2.
- Record the total number of correctly identified pairs in the "Number Correct" box on the test protocol.
- To ensure accuracy when entering scores into the software program, record the number correct in the "Software Score Entry" box on the test protocol.
- Verify that the correct version number (e.g., 1 for Visual Matching 1) is entered when keying score data into the WJ III CPP.

Test 7: Numbers Reversed

Range: 0–30
Scoring Reminders:

- Score correct responses 1, incorrect responses 0.
- All items below the basal are considered correct responses and calculated in the total number correct.
- Record the total number correct and all items below the basal in the "Number Correct" box on the test protocol.

Test 8: Incomplete Words

Range: 0–44
Scoring Reminders:

- Score correct responses 1, incorrect responses 0.
- Words that are pronounced incompletely and/or broken words are considered errors and scored 0.
- Although the test instructions imply that single-word responses are required for credit, acceptable two- and three-word answers are also included in the scoring key.

- Sum all correctly answered items and record this total in the "Number Correct" box on the test protocol.

Test 9: Auditory Working Memory

Range: 0–42
Scoring Reminders:

- Each item is scored 0, 1, or 2.
- A 2-point response requires the examinee to provide the words in the correct order followed by the digits in the correct order.
- A 1-point response requires the examinee to state either the words or the digits in the correct order. The examinee must attempt to state the words first to receive credit.
- Record 0 points when neither the words nor digits are provided in the correct order or when the examinee presents digits before words.
- Mispronunciations resulting from articulation errors, dialect variations, or regional speech patterns are not considered errors.
- Very similar-sounding responses (e.g., "cap" for "cat") or rhyming responses (e.g., "neat" for "meat") are considered correct.
- Record the total points for each item in the space to the left of the item on the test protocol.
- Enter the total number of correctly answered items (and all items below the basal) in the "Number of Points" box on the test protocol.

Test 10: Visual-Auditory Learning–Delayed

Range: 0–123
Scoring Reminders:

- All of Test 2: Visual-Auditory Learning must be administered prior to administering Test 10: Visual-Auditory Learning–Delayed.
- Circle each word the subject misses or is told after a 5-s pause. The number of errors will be used to score this test.
- Omitted words and inserted words are scored as errors.
- For words with two symbols (e.g., "ride . . . ing"), each symbol is con-

sidered separately in scoring. If one part of a two-symbol word is incorrect, score the incorrect part only as an error.

- If an examinee fails to provide a response within 5 s, point to the symbol, say the word, and score the nonresponse as an error.
- Record the total number of errors in the "Number of Errors" box on the test protocol.
- Be sure to record the date and time on the test protocol before administering the test. This information is necessary when entering test data into the WJ III CPP.

Test 11: General Information

Range: 11A, (0–26); 11B, (0–22)
Scoring Reminders:

- Score correct responses 1, incorrect responses 0.
- Mispronunciations resulting from articulation errors, dialect variations, or regional speech patterns are not considered errors.
- English-dominant bilingual examinees should receive credit for correct responses given either in English or another language (examples of correct Spanish responses are provided in the test easel next to each item).
- Record the total number of correct items and all items below the basal in the "Number Correct" box on the test protocol. There are two "Number Correct" boxes, one for Test 11A: General Information–Where and one for Test 11B: General Information–What.
- Record the total number correct in the WJ III CPP for each subtest administered (i.e., Test 11A: General Information–Where and Test 11B: General Information–What).

Test 12: Retrieval Fluency

Range: A (Item 1), 0–60; B (Item 2), 0–60; C (Item 3), 0–60
Scoring Reminders:

- Use tally marks to record the number of correct item responses on the test protocol.

- Duplicate responses are not scored twice.
- English-dominant bilingual examinees are given credit for responses provided in English or another language unless the response is the same in English and the other language (e.g., "milk" *and* "leche").
- Record the total number of correct responses in the "Number Correct" box after each item on the test protocol.
- If the total score for an item exceeds 60, enter 60 as the number correct.
- Record the number correct for each item in the WJ III CPP.

Test 13: Picture Recognition

Range: A, 0–9; B, 0–25; C, 0–41; D, 0–59
Scoring Reminders:

- Score correctly identified pictures 1.
- Score 1 for all correctly identified pictures, regardless of the order in which they are identified.
- If the examinee names more than the requested number of pictures, score only the last pictures identified (e.g., if three pictures must be identified and the examinee names four, score the last three responses given).
- Record the total number of points for a set of items in the corresponding cutoff box provided on the test protocol.
- To ensure accuracy when entering scores into the software program, record the total number of points and the letter corresponding to the block of items administered in the "Software Score Entry" box on the test protocol.

Test 14: Auditory Attention

Range: 0–50
Scoring Reminders:

- Training and sample items must be administered to all examinees.
- Score correct responses 1, incorrect responses 0.

- Record the total number of correct responses in the "Number Correct" box on the test protocol.
- Do not include points for training items or sample items when calculating the total number of correct items.

Test 15: Analysis-Synthesis

Range: A, 0–7; B, 0–19; C, 0–25; D, 0–31; E, 0–35
Scoring Reminders:

- Score correct responses 1, incorrect responses 0.
- The Color Pretest should be administered to all examinees. If the examinee is unable to be trained on the Color Pretest, note this by checking the "Untrainable" box on the test protocol.
- Do not score the test for examinees who cannot be trained due to color discrimination or identification difficulties.
- Record the total number correct for a set of items in the corresponding cutoff box provided on the test protocol.
- Do not include points for pretest, introductory, or sample items when calculating the total number correct.
- To ensure accuracy when entering scores into the software program, record the number correct and the letter corresponding to the block of items administered in the "Software Score Entry" box on the test protocol.

Test 16: Decision Speed

Range: 0–40
Scoring Reminders:

- Score correctly identified pairs 1.
- Use the Decision Speed scoring template to score the test.
- Examinees must circle two pictures to receive points.
- Record a score of 0 for circled items that are only loosely related (e.g., two things that may be found in a house).
- Do not include sample items and practice exercises in the total number correct.

- Record the total number of points for items answered within the 3-min time limit in the "Number Correct" box on the protocol.

Test 17: Memory for Words

Range: 0–24
Scoring Reminders:

- Score correct responses 1, incorrect responses 0.
- Examinees must repeat words in the exact order presented to receive credit.
- Very similar-sounding responses (e.g., "cap" for "cat") or rhyming responses (e.g., "neat" for "meat") are considered correct.
- Mispronunciations resulting from articulation errors, dialect variations, or regional speech patterns are not considered errors.
- Record the total number of points, including all items below the basal, in the "Number Correct" box on the test protocol.

Test 18: Rapid Picture Naming

Range: 0–120
Scoring Reminders:

- Score correct responses 1, incorrect responses 0.
- If the examinee provides a synonym (e.g., "puppy" for "dog") score the response correct. However, if the examinee provides a word that is similar in meaning but is not a synonym (e.g., "cup" for "glass") score the response incorrect.
- Mispronunciations resulting from articulation errors, dialect variations, or regional speech patterns are not considered errors.
- English-dominant bilingual examinees should receive credit for correct responses given either in English or another language (examples of correct Spanish responses are provided in the test easel next to each item).
- Record the total completion time, in minutes and seconds, in the "Time" boxes of the protocol. There is a 2-min time limit for this test.

- Record the total number of correct responses in the "Number Correct" box on the test protocol.

Test 19: Planning

Range: Depends on which set of items is administered
Scoring Reminders:

- Record the total number of errors for each item on the test protocol.
- Each segment within an item is a potential error. Segments are delineated by color and separated by space.
- Retraced or uncompleted segments are considered errors.
- Sum the total number of errors for each page of items and record the total in the corresponding cutoff box on the test protocol.
- To ensure accuracy when entering scores into the software program, record the number of errors in the box corresponding to the block of items administered in the "Software Score Entry" box on the test protocol.
- If a particular block of items was not administered, place an "X" in the "Software Score Entry" box for those items.

Test 20: Pair Cancellation

Range: 0–69
Scoring Reminders:

- Score 1 for correctly identified pairs.
- Use the Pair Cancellation scoring template to score this test.
- To receive credit, the circled pair must consist of a ball followed by a dog in the same row.
- A correctly circled ball-dog pair that includes part of an adjacent figure is considered a correct response. However, if the other figure is included in its entirety, consider the response incorrect.
- A partially circled pair that does not include all of the dog or all of the ball is considered correct, as long as the intent is clear.
- A circle around a correctly chosen pair that overlaps with another circle is considered correct.

- Ignore responses in which an examinee circles a ball at the end of one row with a dog at the beginning of another row.
- If an examinee crosses out a correctly circled pair, consider the item incorrect.
- Do not include points for sample or practice items when calculating the total number correct.
- Record the total completion time, in minutes and seconds, in the "Time" section of the protocol. There is a 3-min time limit for this test.
- Record the total number of correctly circled pairs that were identified within the 3-min time limit, in the "Number Correct" box on the test protocol.

🐾 TEST YOURSELF 🐾

1. **When querying responses, you should use the Test Book query key. If an item does not have a query key, *do not* query that item.** True or False?

2. **When an examinee provides multiple responses to an item, only one of which is correct, you should give credit for the correct response.** True or False?

3. **If an examinee provides an incorrect response for the first part of a two-symbol word on Test 2: Visual-Auditory Learning, you should**

   (a) consider the response an error and record a score of 0.

   (b) consider the response correct and record a score of 1.

   (c) consider each symbol separately; record a score of 1 if the second part is correct.

   (d) query the examinee and ask him or her to attempt the word again.

4. **For which of the following test(s) are synonyms considered an acceptable response?**

   (a) Visual-Auditory Learning.

   (b) Concept Formation.

   (c) Both a and b.

   (d) None of the above. If an examinee provides a synonym in response to an item (e.g., says "little" for "small"), the response is considered an error.

(continued)

5. **If an examiner inadvertently exceeds the time limit for any of the timed tests, that test must not be scored and should be declared invalid.** True or False?

6. **The raw score for which of the following test(s) is based on the total number of errors committed?**

   (a) Test 2: Visual-Auditory Learning

   (b) Test 10: Visual-Auditory Learning–Delayed

   (c) Test 19: Planning

   (d) All of the above

7. **On Test 19: Planning, responses should be scored by examining the accuracy of the individual line segments comprising the patterns.** True or False?

8. **Examiners should ensure that all sample items are included in the calculation of raw scores.** True or False?

9. **On Test 12: Retrieval Fluency, an English-dominant bilingual examinee should be given credit in which of the following situations?**

   (a) The examinee provides a correct response in English.

   (b) The examinee provides a correct response in Spanish.

   (c) The examinee provides a correct response in English and later provides the same response in Spanish.

   (d) Both a and b.

10. **Examiners have the option of calculating all cluster scores either by hand or by using the WJ III Compuscore and Profiles Program.** True or False?

Answers: 1. False; 2. False; 3. c; 4. b; 5. False; 6. d; 7. True; 8. False; 9. d; 10. False

Four

HOW TO INTERPRET THE WJ III COG

OVERVIEW

The WJ III COG was designed to reflect the body of research on the structure of human cognitive abilities known as Cattell-Horn-Carroll (CHC) theory. CHC theory is based on an integration of two independently derived theories of intellectual abilities: *Gf-Gc* theory and Carroll's three-stratum theory.

Gf-Gc theory is a model that has been developed and refined over the last 60 years by Cattell, Horn, and their research associates. At an American Psychological Association conference in 1941, Cattell proposed that the constructs of fluid intelligence (*Gf*) and crystallized intelligence (*Gc*) could be distinguished as two basic types of human intellectual ability. As a result of this early conceptualization, this theory came to be called *Gf-Gc* theory (Horn, 1965, 1991; Horn & Noll, 1997) even though the theory has subsequently been expanded to include as many as 9 or 10 broad factors.

Carroll's (1993) three-stratum theory is based on exploratory factor analyses of more than 400 data sets of human cognitive ability experiments. Carroll developed the three-stratum theory to describe both the content and the hierarchical structure of cognitive abilities. Each stratum represents a different level of abstraction. Stratum I includes approximately 70 narrow abilities derived from more than 400 data sets; Stratum II represents Carroll's groupings of differentiated broad abilities that are highly similar to the *Gf-Gc* factors recognized by Horn and others; Stratum III represents the construct of general intellectual ability (*g*) (Carroll, 1993, 1998). Figure 4.1 is a pictographic representation of Carroll's three-stratum theory.

By mutual consensus, the integration of these two independently and empirically derived theories was named CHC theory (J. P. Carroll & J. L. Horn, personal communication, July 1999). CHC theory provided the blueprint for

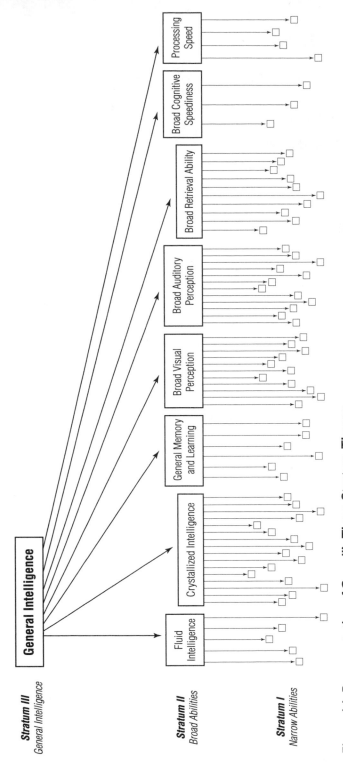

Figure 4.1 Representation of Carroll's Three-Stratum Theory

Stratum III
General Intelligence

Stratum II
Broad Abilities

Stratum I
Narrow Abilities

General Intelligence

Processing Speed

Broad Cognitive Speediness

Broad Retrieval Ability

Broad Auditory Perception

Broad Visual Perception

General Memory and Learning

Crystallized Intelligence

Fluid Intelligence

the WJ III and provides support for interpretation of the WJ III COG at three levels: general intellectual ability, several broad cognitive abilities, and specific (or narrow) cognitive abilities.

The Three Strata in the WJ III COG

The WJ III COG includes scores representing all three strata of CHC theory. At Stratum III, the General Intellectual Ability (GIA) score is a measure of the first-principal component (g). As will be explained, the GIA score does not represent a distinct cognitive ability. Also, it is both similar to and different from an IQ score or overall composite score obtained from other intelligence batteries.

The WJ III GIA score is a measure of psychometric g, one of psychology's oldest and most solidly established constructs—and the first authentic latent variable in the history of psychology. The existence of g was originally hypothesized by Galton (1869) and was later empirically established by Spearman (1904). It is important to note that g (and by inference, the GIA scores) does not represent an ability per se; rather, it is a distillation of abilities. Unlike the broad and narrow abilities identified by CHC theory, g simply cannot be described in terms of information content. There is no singular, defining characteristic of g that can be stated in psychological terms. You should consider the GIA score as an index of a well-defined theoretical postulate (g) that is identified as Stratum III in Carroll's three-stratum model of human cognitive abilities (Carroll, 1993). The index has broad practical application, as g will often be the best *single-score* predictor of various global criteria such as overall school achievement or other life outcomes that have some relationship to cognitive ability.

The GIA score is an index of the common variance among the broad and narrow cognitive abilities measured by the component tests in the WJ III COG. It is a distillate of several cognitive abilities and the primary source of variance that is common to all of the tests included in its calculation. Some scholars of intelligence, notably Horn, state that g is merely a statistical artifact. Others, such as Jensen (1998) refer to g as a property of cognitive processing. For example, Jensen said that g "reflects individual differences in information processing as manifested in functions such as attending, selecting, searching, internalizing, deciding, discriminating, generalizing, learning, remembering, and using incoming and past-acquired information to solve problems and cope with the exigencies of the environment" (p. 117).

Overall scores from other intelligence test batteries (such as IQ scores) are not distillate measures of psychometric g. An IQ or other full-scale score is an aggregate of the standardized scores on a set of subtests that comprise the scale, not a distillate of general intellectual ability. Rather, IQ, composite, or overall scores are an arbitrary mix of different test scores, the selection of which varies according to the orientation of each test's authors or publisher. Spearman (1927) called such scores a "hotch pot." However, it is important to note that most IQ or similar composite scores are highly correlated with g. As a general rule, the greater the breadth of cognitive abilities measured by an intelligence battery, the higher the overall score will correlate with g. Consequently, the overall scores from other intelligence tests correlate fairly well with g as operationalized by the WJ III GIA scores.

In the WJ III COG, computer scoring makes calculation of general intellectual ability, or g, possible. Each test included in the GIA score is weighted, as a function of age, to provide the best estimate of g. In general, the tests that measure Gc (Test 1: Verbal Comprehension and Test 11: General Information) and Gf (Test 5: Concept Formation and Test 15: Analysis-Synthesis) are among the highest g-weighted tests, a finding that is consistent with the extant factor-analytic research on g (e.g., Carroll, 1993). Table 4.1 provides the average GIA weights for selected age groups and demonstrates that the g weights for the individual tests do not vary much by age.

In CHC theory, the broad abilities represent Stratum II. In the WJ III COG, the clusters representing the broad abilities provide the most important information for analysis of within-individual variability. These scores provide the best level of interpretive information for determining patterns of educationally and psychologically relevant strengths and weaknesses. The WJ III COG was designed to provide greater breadth of narrow abilities in each broad cognitive ability score. To enhance validity (generalizability) of the cluster, each component test was designed to measure a different aspect of the broad ability. In clinical assessment, when significant score differences are found to exist between tests that comprise a broad ability, diagnostic interpretation is enhanced through a distinction between performance on tests measuring the narrow abilities. The following description of the broad (Stratum II) abilities includes information on the narrow (Stratum I) abilities included in each broad ability score.

Table 4.1 General Intellectual Ability (GIA) Average g Weights by Age Group

	Age																								
	2	3	4	5	6	7	8	9	10	11	12	13	14	15	16	17	18	19	20–29	30–39	40–49	50–59	60–69	70–79	80+
General Intellectual Ability–Std																									
Verbal Comprehension	.19	.20	.20	.20	.20	.20	.20	.20	.20	.20	.20	.20	.20	.20	.20	.19	.19	.19	.18	.17	.17	.17	.17	.17	.17
Visual-Auditory Learning	.16	.16	.16	.16	.16	.16	.17	.17	.17	.17	.17	.17	.17	.17	.17	.16	.16	.16	.16	.16	.16	.17	.17	.17	.17
Spatial Relations	.10	.10	.10	.10	.09	.09	.09	.09	.09	.09	.09	.09	.09	.09	.10	.10	.11	.11	.13	.12	.11	.11	.10	.10	.10
Sound Blending	.11	.11	.11	.11	.11	.12	.12	.12	.12	.12	.12	.12	.12	.12	.12	.12	.12	.12	.12	.12	.12	.12	.11	.11	.10
Concept Formation	.17	.17	.18	.18	.18	.18	.18	.19	.19	.19	.19	.19	.19	.19	.19	.19	.19	.18	.18	.17	.17	.16	.15	.15	.15
Visual Matching	.10	.10	.10	.10	.10	.10	.10	.10	.10	.10	.10	.10	.10	.10	.10	.10	.10	.10	.11	.13	.14	.14	.15	.15	.15
Numbers Reversed	.17	.16	.16	.15	.15	.14	.14	.13	.13	.13	.13	.13	.13	.13	.13	.13	.13	.13	.13	.13	.14	.14	.14	.15	.16
General Intellectual Ability–Ext																									
Verbal Comprehension	.11	.11	.11	.12	.12	.12	.12	.12	.13	.13	.13	.13	.13	.13	.12	.12	.12	.12	.12	.11	.10	.10	.10	.10	.10
Visual-Auditory Learning	.08	.08	.09	.09	.09	.09	.09	.09	.09	.09	.09	.09	.09	.09	.09	.09	.08	.08	.08	.08	.09	.09	.09	.09	.09
Spatial Relations	.04	.04	.05	.05	.05	.05	.05	.05	.05	.05	.05	.05	.05	.05	.05	.05	.06	.06	.06	.06	.05	.05	.05	.05	.06
Sound Blending	.06	.06	.06	.06	.06	.06	.06	.06	.06	.06	.07	.07	.07	.07	.07	.07	.07	.07	.07	.07	.06	.06	.06	.06	.06
Concept Formation	.08	.08	.09	.09	.10	.10	.10	.10	.11	.11	.11	.11	.11	.11	.11	.11	.11	.11	.10	.09	.09	.08	.08	.08	.07
Visual Matching	.06	.06	.06	.06	.06	.06	.06	.06	.06	.06	.06	.06	.06	.06	.06	.06	.06	.06	.07	.07	.08	.08	.08	.08	.09
Numbers Reversed	.08	.08	.08	.08	.08	.07	.07	.07	.07	.07	.07	.07	.07	.07	.07	.07	.07	.07	.07	.07	.08	.07	.07	.08	.08
General Information	.09	.09	.09	.10	.10	.10	.10	.10	.11	.11	.11	.11	.11	.11	.11	.11	.11	.11	.10	.10	.09	.09	.09	.09	.09
Retrieval Fluency	.07	.07	.07	.07	.07	.07	.07	.07	.06	.06	.06	.06	.06	.06	.05	.05	.05	.05	.05	.07	.08	.07	.07	.06	.06
Picture Recognition	.04	.04	.03	.03	.03	.03	.03	.03	.03	.03	.03	.03	.03	.03	.03	.03	.03	.03	.04	.04	.04	.05	.05	.05	.05
Auditory Attention	.07	.06	.06	.05	.05	.04	.04	.04	.03	.03	.03	.03	.03	.03	.03	.03	.03	.03	.03	.04	.05	.05	.05	.05	.05
Analysis-Synthesis	.08	.08	.08	.08	.08	.08	.09	.09	.09	.09	.09	.09	.09	.09	.09	.09	.09	.09	.09	.08	.08	.08	.08	.09	.09
Decision Speed	.08	.08	.08	.07	.07	.06	.06	.06	.06	.05	.05	.05	.05	.05	.05	.05	.05	.05	.05	.06	.06	.07	.08	.08	.08
Memory for Words	.05	.05	.05	.05	.05	.06	.06	.06	.06	.06	.06	.06	.06	.06	.06	.06	.06	.06	.07	.06	.06	.05	.04	.04	.04

Source: Adapted from WJ III Technical Manual, pp. 153–154, Riverside Publishing 2001.

Comprehension-Knowledge (*Gc*), sometimes called crystallized intelligence, includes the breadth and depth of a person's acquired knowledge, the ability to communicate one's knowledge (especially verbally), and the ability to reason using previously learned experiences or procedures. The *Gc* factor includes two tests measuring different narrow abilities. Test 1: Verbal Comprehension primarily measures *lexical knowledge* and *language development*. Test 11: General Information primarily measures *general verbal information*. In the WJ III COG, this cluster is also called *Verbal Ability*.

Long-Term Retrieval (*Glr*) is the ability to store information and fluently retrieve it later. The *Glr* factor includes two tests, each measuring a different aspect of retrieval—Test 2: Visual-Auditory Learning measures *associative memory* and Test 12: Retrieval Fluency measures *ideational fluency*.

Visual-Spatial Thinking (*Gv*) is the ability to perceive, analyze, synthesize, and think with visual patterns, including the ability to store and recall visual representations. The *Gv* factor includes two tests, Test 3: Spatial Relations and Test 13: Picture Recognition. Spatial Relations measures the ability to use *visualization* in thinking, whereas Picture Recognition is a *visual memory* task.

Auditory Processing (*Ga*) is the ability to analyze, synthesize, and discriminate auditory stimuli, including the ability to process and discriminate speech sounds that may be presented under distorted conditions. Auditory Processing includes *phonetic coding* (measured by Test 4: Sound Blending) and the ability to understand speech that has been distorted or masked in one or more ways (or *resistance to auditory stimulus distortion*). These abilities are measured by Test 14: Auditory Attention.

Fluid Reasoning (*Gf*) is the ability to reason, form concepts, and solve problems using unfamiliar information or novel procedures. The *Gf* cluster includes two tests of fluid reasoning. Test 5: Concept Formation is a test of *induction* and Test 15: Analysis-Synthesis measures *sequential reasoning*.

Processing Speed (*Gs*) is the ability to perform automatic cognitive tasks, an aspect of cognitive efficiency. Test 6: Visual Matching measures *perceptual speed* and Test 16: Decision Speed measures *speed of semantic processing*.

Short-Term Memory (*Gsm*) is the ability to apprehend and hold information in immediate awareness and then use it within a few seconds. The *Gsm* factor includes two tests: Test 7: Numbers Reversed is a complex measure of *working memory capacity*, and Test 17: Memory for Words is a verbal *memory span* test.

Rapid Reference 4.1 provides an overview of the broad and narrow abilities

≡ Rapid Reference 4.1

Broad Factors and Narrow Abilities Measured by the WJ III Tests of Cognitive Abilities

Broad CHC Factor	Standard Battery Primary Narrow Abilities Measured		Extended Battery Primary Narrow Abilities Measured	
Comprehension-Knowledge (Gc)	Test 1:	Verbal Comprehension *Lexical Knowledge* *Language Development*	Test 11:	General Information *General (Verbal) Information*
Long-Term Retrieval (Glr)	Test 2:	Visual-Auditory Learning *Associative Memory*	Test 12:	Retrieval Fluency *Ideational Fluency*
	Test 10:	Visual-Auditory Learning-Delayed *Associative Memory*		
Visual-Spatial Thinking (Gv)	Test 3:	Spatial Relations *Visualization* *Spatial Relations*	Test 13:	Picture Recognition *Visual Memory*
			Test 19:	Planning *Spatial Scanning* *General Sequential Reasoning*
Auditory Processing (Ga)	Test 4:	Sound Blending *Phonetic Coding: Synthesis*	Test 14:	Auditory Attention *Speech-Sound Discrimination* *Resistance to Auditory Stimulus Distortion*
	Test 8:	Incomplete Words *Phonetic Coding: Analysis*		

Broad CHC Factor	Standard Battery Primary Narrow Abilities Measured	Extended Battery Primary Narrow Abilities Measured
Fluid Reasoning (Gf)	Test 5: Concept Formation *Induction*	Test 15: Analysis-Synthesis *General Sequential Reasoning* Test 19: Planning *Spatial Scanning* *General Sequential Reasoning*
Processing Speed (Gs)	Test 6: Visual Matching *Perceptual Speed*	Test 16: Decision Speed *Semantic Processing Speed* Test 18: Rapid Picture Naming *Naming Facility* Test 20: Pair Cancellation *Attention and Concentration*
Short-Term Memory (Gsm)	Test 7: Numbers Reversed *Working Memory* Test 9: Auditory Working Memory *Working Memory*	Test 17: Memory for Words *Memory Span*

Source: Adapted from *WJ III Technical Manual*, p. 13, Riverside Publishing 2001.

measured by the WJ III COG. Knowledge of both broad and narrow abilities that make up the WJ III COG factor scores will enable you to interpret test results in a meaningful and useful way. Appendix A is a glossary of CHC abilities measured by the WJ III COG.

Other Interpretive Clusters

The WJ III COG tests can be combined into other clusters to provide additional interpretive information about an individual's performance on the WJ III. These clusters include Verbal Ability, Thinking Ability, Cognitive Efficiency, Cognitive Fluency, Phonemic Awareness, Working Memory, Broad Attention, and Executive Processes.

Three of these clusters (Verbal Ability, Thinking Ability, and Cognitive Efficiency) represent broad, hierarchical categories of cognitive abilities that influence what we observe in an individual's cognitive or academic performance. These categories are represented in Figure 4.2. Each of the three categories is comprised of abilities that contribute in a common way to per-

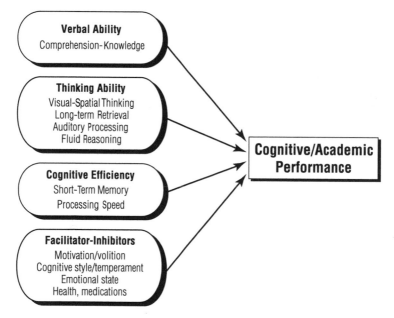

Figure 4.2 WJ III COG Performance Model

Source: Adapted from *WJ III Tests of Cognitive Abilities Examiner's Manual,* p. 78, Riverside Publishing 2001.

formance, but contribute differently from the common contributions of the other categories.

Verbal Ability represents higher-order language-based acquired knowledge and the ability to communicate that knowledge. This cluster correlates very highly with verbal scales from other intelligence batteries. The *Thinking Ability* cluster represents a sampling of the different thinking processes (Long-Term Retrieval, Visual-Spatial Thinking, Auditory Processing, and Fluid Reasoning). These abilities are involved when information in short-term memory cannot be processed automatically. Comparisons among the different thinking abilities may provide clues to any preferred learning styles or evidence of specific difficulties. The *Cognitive Efficiency* cluster provides a sampling of two different automatic cognitive processes—processing speed and short-term memory, both of which are needed for complex cognitive functioning. A fourth category, Facilitator-Inhibitors, represents a group of noncognitive variables, such as motivation, personality style, and health, that also influence cognitive performance.

The *Cognitive Fluency* cluster is a measure of cognitive automaticity, or the speed with which an individual performs simple to complex cognitive tasks. Interpretation of this cluster is related to Carroll's (1993) distinction between tests of level versus rate. The three tests that comprise this cluster (Test 12: Retrieval Fluency, Test 16: Decision Speed, and Test 18: Rapid Picture Naming) are all measures of rate of performance rather than level of ability. For example, Rapid Picture Naming measures rate of *naming facility,* a narrow CHC ability. The Cognitive Fluency cluster can provide important information when compared to the *Academic Fluency* cluster from the WJ III ACH, or to other cognitive tests measuring the level of performance, rather than the rate of performance, of the same broad cognitive ability.

The WJ III COG includes a *Phonemic Awareness* cluster. This cluster measures the ability to attend to the sound structure of language through analyzing and synthesizing speech sounds, a narrow CHC ability. This ability is important in early reading and spelling acquisition. Because scores on phonemic awareness measures often co-vary with reading achievement scores, the Phonemic Awareness cluster can provide important diagnostic information about reading success or failure.

Certain WJ III COG tests provide indicators of an individual's executive functions, including attention and working memory. Inferences based on the processing characteristics of the tasks, along with clinical and factor-analytic research on the WJ III tests and on similar measures from other batteries, support interpretation of some of the WJ III COG tests as measures of executive functioning.

On all of the WJ III COG executive processing, attention, and working memory tests, evaluation of a subject's performance can be aided by careful analysis of the processes, and by subsequent comparison of performance across measures. Rapid Reference 4.2 contains a list of the working memory, attention, and executive processing tasks contained in several WJ III COG tests. The table identifies the key executive functions measured by each test, the nature of the stimuli, the cognitive processes used in performance of the task, and the response modalities. When attempting to measure any executive processing function (e.g., working memory, attention), it is important to consider the multidimensional nature of the task. For example, a cancellation task, such as the Pair Cancellation test, involves several abilities: sustained attention, processing speed, motoric speed, as well as executive functioning. High or low performance could be attributed to any of these abilities.

Several of these tests and clusters may provide additional information about the cognitive characteristics of individuals with learning disabilities, Attention-Deficit Hyperactivity Disorder (ADHD), and certain acquired etiologies, such as traumatic brain injury. For example, deficits in executive functioning are often observed in an inability to allocate and sustain attentional resources (Denckla, 1989). The *Broad Attention* cluster provides a cognitive index of attention. Considered individually, however, each of the four tests that comprise the Broad Attention cluster taps a qualitatively different cognitive aspect of attention. Significant differences among test scores that comprise this cluster may reveal individual patterns of variability in cognition. Attentional capacity, or the ability to hold information while performing some action on the information, is required by Test 7: Numbers Reversed. Sustained attention, or the capacity to stay on task in a vigilant manner, is required by Test 20: Pair Cancellation. Test 14: Auditory Attention requires selective attention, or the ability to focus attentional resources when distracting stimuli are present. Test 9: Auditory Working Memory requires the ability to rearrange information placed in short-term memory to form two distinct sequences. Test 9: Auditory Working Memory and Test 7: Numbers Reversed may also be combined to form a Working Memory cluster, which measures

≡Rapid Reference 4.2

Executive Functions and Processing Characteristics of the WJ III COG Tests Measuring Working Memory, Attention, and Executive Processes

Test	Key Executive Functions	Stimuli	Task Analysis Process	Response
Test 7: Numbers Reversed	Working Memory Attentional Capacity	Verbal/Auditory	Transformation	Verbal/Oral
Test 9: Auditory Working Memory	Working Memory Divided Attention	Verbal/Auditory	Reorganization Sorting Sequencing	Verbal/Oral
Test 14: Auditory Attention	Selective Attention	Verbal/Auditory	Discrimination	Nonverbal/Motor
Test 20: Pair Cancellation	Sustained Attention	Nonverbal/Visual	Recognition Monitoring	Nonverbal/Motor
Test 19: Planning	Planning	Nonverbal/Visual-Spatial	Forethought	Nonverbal/Motor
Test 5: Concept Formation	Concept Shifting	Nonverbal/Visual	Categorization	Verbal/Oral

Source: Adapted from WJ III Tests of Cognitive Abilities Examiner's Manual, p. 86, Riverside Publishing 2001.

the ability to hold information in immediate awareness while performing a mental operation on it.

Most models of executive functioning also posit a central executive or processing mechanism that coordinates and manages the activities and processes in working memory. The *Executive Processes* cluster may measure certain aspects of the central executive, such as the response inhibition, cognitive flexibility, and the planning functions identified by Pennington (1997). Response inhibition and interference control are required by the Test 20: Pair Cancellation. Because the test is a timed task, it also provides information about the subject's ability to perform a simple cognitive task under time pressure. Test 5: Concept Formation requires the ability to shift one's mental set. Careful observation of the ease with which the subject makes conceptual transformations provides important clinical information.

The neuropsychological construct of executive functioning is derived, in part, from task analyses of certain types of psychological tests and inferences made about the processing characteristics needed to perform the tasks (Borkowski & Burke, 1996). Test 19: Planning provides an example of this process.

The concept for the Planning test was based on an historical puzzle from Prussia called the Bridges of Königsberg. This city (now in Russia and renamed Kaliningrad) had seven bridges connecting different combinations of four pieces of land (two riverbanks, a peninsula, and an island). The puzzle was to walk around Königsberg, crossing all seven bridges, but crossing each of the bridges only once. Eventually it was determined that the Bridges of Königsberg puzzle could not be solved, but for centuries it kept citizens and visitors alike planning different routes to solve the problem.

Unlike the Bridges of Königsberg, each of the items on the Planning test has a solution. In this test, the individual is presented with a series of items, or puzzles, and is asked to trace the pattern without lifting the pencil from the paper or retracing any lines. Following a number of sample exercises, the individual is presented with the test items, arranged in order of difficulty. Figure 4.3 presents a simulated item of intermediate difficulty. Solutions to these tasks draw primarily upon visual-spatial thinking ability, employing the narrow ability of spatial scanning. Because the tasks are complex and novel, the test also draws upon fluid reasoning abilities.

As in all tests purported to measure aspects of executive functioning, your

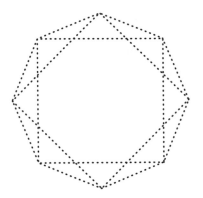

Figure 4.3 Simulated Item from the WJ III COG Planning Test

observations are critical in providing qualitative information about an individual's performance. Individuals who begin these tasks impulsively, using a trial and error approach, or who lack a cognitive capacity for sustained attention, typically don't perform well. Individuals who do perform well usually demonstrate a pattern of careful observation and reflection. Periods of reflection are the essential components of planning as they provide an opportunity for (a) the development of an operational framework, (b) the generation and consideration of alternative hypotheses, (c) the sequencing of responses in an orderly fashion, and (d) the revision or modification of proposed plans of action.

Available Scores

The WJ III Compuscore and Profiles Program (WJ III CPP; Schrank & Woodcock, 2001) calculates all derived scores and provides several options for score interpretation. The WJ III CPP includes both age and grade norms. That is, each individual's performance on the WJ III can be compared to peers of the same age or in the same grade. An *age equivalent* reflects the age level in the norming sample at which the average score is the same as the individual's score. Similarly, a *grade equivalent* reflects the grade level in the norming sample at which the average score is the same as the individual's score.

Age- and grade-equivalent scores are not standards of performance. They describe nothing more than the correspondence, in terms of the number of

Test 7   Numbers Reversed
Scoring Table
Encircle row for the Number Correct.

Number Correct	Age Equivalents	Grade Equivalents
0	<5-0	<K.0
1	5-0	<K.0
2	5-1	<K.0
3	5-3	<K.0
4	5-4	<K.0
5	5-8	K.3
6	6-1	1.0
7	6-6	1.5
8	6-11	2.0
9	7-6	2.4
10	8-2	3.0
11	9-3	3.8
12	10-7	5.0
13	12-2	6.6
14	13-11	8.3
15	15-8	10.4
16	17-4	12.9
17	19	13.0
18	>22	15.4
>18	>22	>18.0

Note: Age equivalents and grade equivalents are estimates of the precise valves provided by the software scoring program.

Figure 4.4 Scoring Table for Numbers Reversed

Source: Adapted from *WJ III Tests of Cognitive Abilities* Test Record, p. 11, Riverside Publishing 2001.

raw score points obtained, between the individual and the average performance of the age or grade group defined by the age- or grade-equivalent score. Figure 4.4 shows the scoring table for Test 7: Numbers Reversed. The row corresponding to a raw score of 10 is circled for an individual aged 14 years, 9 months (14-9) that was administered this test. This individual's raw score on Numbers Reversed is comparable to the raw score obtained by the average individual at age 8-2 (and grade 3.0) in the normative sample. Unlike the age- and grade-equivalent scores obtained from many tests on the WJ III ACH, age- and grade-equivalent scores on the WJ III COG cannot be readily equated to an instructional level. They do, however, provide information related to the development level in this ability demonstrated by the subject. In this example, the age equivalent of 8-2 tells us that this individual did not perform as well as the average individual at age 9-3. But without further information, we do not know if there are any practical implications of that obtained score.

The individual's standard scores, percentile ranks, and relative proficiency indices will be affected by the normative basis (age or grade) selected. Age norms range from 2 to 90+; grade norms range from K.0 to the beginning of the second year of graduate school. The choice of age or grade norms depends on the purpose of the assessment. In some instances, when an individual is older or younger than his or her grade peers, grade norms are the more appropriate comparison because the students in the same grade are the most relevant peer group. In other instances, age norms are required. For example, eligibility requirements for some state special education programs specify the use of age-based norms for determining discrepancies between ability and achievement. Age norms are also more appropriate for individuals not attending school, such as preschool children or adults.

The *Relative Proficiency Index* (RPI) is a score that allows you to make statements about the individual's expected level of proficiency on tasks that are similar to those on the test. This score is a variation of the index that is used with Snellen charts to describe visual acuity. In the Snellen Index, a person with 20/40 vision can distinguish at 20 feet what another person with normal vision can distinguish at 40 feet. An RPI of 90/90 conveys that an individual is predicted to demonstrate with 90% proficiency those tasks that an average individual in the age- or grade-based comparison group also would demonstrate with 90% proficiency.

The WJ III CPP also calculates percentile ranks and standard scores. You have the option of reporting a 68%, 90%, or 95% confidence band around the obtained standard score. The *percentile rank* (PR) indicates the percentage of individuals in the age- or grade-based standardization group that obtained a score as low or lower than the individual being assessed. Like the percentile ranks, WJ III *standard scores* are peer comparison scores. The WJ III standard scores have a mean of 100 and a standard deviation of 15. This allows comparison between WJ III scores and scores obtained on tests that use the same mean and standard deviation. On the WJ III, it is possible to obtain standard scores less than 1. In certain instances, standard scores greater than 200 can be obtained.

The WJ III CPP also includes a number of additional score options. For each test, you can elect to report a W score (a special transformation of the Rasch ability scale), *or* for most tests, you can report a raw score. The W score is on an equal-interval scale and has certain advantages, such as the ability to provide score averages. Additionally, you can elect to report a grade equivalent (if the test was scored using age norms), an age equivalent (if the test was scored using grade norms), a z score, T score, Stanine, NCE (Normal Curve Equivalent), or CALP level. Table 4.2 shows a typical report of scores from the WJ III CPP.

Interpretation of Delayed Recall—Visual-Auditory Learning z Scores

The Visual-Auditory Learning test includes a Delayed Recall (DR) component. Test 10: Visual Auditory Learning–Delayed may be administered from 30 minutes to 8 days later. The z score is used to report the discrepancy between predicted and actual DR scores.

Interpretation of DR test results is based on the difference between the obtained DR score and a predicted DR score. The predicted score is derived from three pieces of information: the subject's age or grade, the initial test score, and the time between administration of the initial and delayed tests. This difference is evaluated in the same manner as an ability/achievement discrepancy. The objective is to determine whether the subject's DR score is within normal limits given age or grade, initial score, and delay interval. The reported statistic is the z score. To show z scores in the Score Report, select the Options tab and then the Report Options tab. The Additional Score Column allows you to select the type of score to be reported in the last column of the Score Report. Choose "z score" and click OK.

A z score indicates the number of standard deviation units (more accurately called standard error of estimate units) separating the predicted and actual scores. This statistic corresponds to the "SD" score reported in the Discrepancies section of the Score Report. A negative z indicates that the delayed score was less than predicted and a positive z indicates that the delayed score was higher than predicted. Scores between -1.00 (PR = 16) and $+1.00$ (PR = 84) are considered "within normal limits." You may, however, use other criteria. For example, -1.30 (PR = 10) and $+1.30$ (PR = 90); -1.50 (PR = 7) and $+1.50$ (PR = 93); or -2.0 (PR = 2) and $+2.00$ (PR = 98).

Table 4.2 WJ III CPP Table of Scores: Woodcock-Johnson III Tests of Cognitive Abilities

CLUSTER/Test	RAW	AE	EASY to DIFF		RPI	PR	SS(68% BAND)	GE
GIA (Ext)	–	9-11	8-3	12-5	76/90	19	87 (85-89)	4.6
VERBAL ABILITY (Ext)	–	8-11	7-6	10-7	56/90	11	82 (78-86)	3.6
THINKING ABILITY (Ext)	–	9-2	7-0	14-3	80/90	17	86 (83-89)	3.7
COG EFFICIENCY (Ext)	–	13-1	11-2	15-10	93/90	62	104 (100-109)	7.7
COMP-KNOWLEDGE (Gc)	–	8-11	7-6	10-7	56/90	11	82 (78-86)	3.6
L-T RETRIEVAL (Glr)	–	7-7	5-4	13-10	78/90	5	75 (70-79)	2.1
VIS-SPATIAL THINK (Gv)	–	11-2	7-4	>25	88/90	43	97 (93-102)	6.1
AUDITORY PROCESS (Ga)	–	15-5	9-7	>25	93/90	68	107 (101-112)	10.4
FLUID REASONING (Gf)	–	7-8	6-9	8-11	44/90	7	77 (74-81)	2.3
PROCESS SPEED (Gs)	–	12-9	11-4	14-8	93/90	58	103 (99-107)	7.5
SHORT-TERM MEM (Gsm)	–	13-8	10-10	17-7	94/90	60	104 (98-109)	8.1
PHONEMIC AWARE	–	13-10	8-11	>28	92/90	60	104 (99-109)	8.7
WORKING MEMORY	–	11-2	9-3	13-8	84/90	39	96 (91-100)	5.7
BROAD ATTENTION	–	13-5	10-9	17-5	93/90	67	106 (102-111)	8.1
COGNITIVE FLUENCY	–	11-8	9-8	14-6	87/90	43	97 (94-100)	6.6
EXEC PROCESSES	–	11-7	9-0	15-9	88/90	43	97 (94-100)	6.0

Verbal Comprehension	-	8-7	7-3	10-2	48/90	10	81 (76-85)	3.1
Visual-Auditory Learning	27-E	7-1	5-7	9-8	64/90	6	76 (73-80)	1.6
Spatial Relations	60-D	8-5	6-1	15-0	80/90	25	90 (86-94)	3.4
Sound Blending	22	15-1	10-6	>26	94/90	64	105 (100-110)	9.9
Concept Formation	14-D	7-3	6-4	8-4	31/90	8	79 (75-83)	2.0
Visual Matching	45-2	12-2	11-1	13-7	89/90	49	100 (95-104)	7.0
Numbers Reversed	13	12-2	9-10	14-10	90/90	50	100 (94-105)	6.6
Incomplete Words	22	11-10	7-0	>33	90/90	48	99 (91-107)	6.5
Auditory Work Memory	18	10-5	8-10	12-6	77/90	30	92 (88-96)	4.9
Vis-Aud Learn—Delayed	42	-	-	-	-	-	-	-
General Information	-	9-4	7-10	11-2	63/90	17	86 (80-91)	4.1
Retrieval Fluency	53	9-5	4-11	>30	87/90	22	88 (82-95)	3.8
Picture Recognition	51-D	16-9	9-4	>25	94/90	65	106 (100-112)	11.1
Auditory Attention	40	17-3	8-6	>20	93/90	65	106 (98-114)	12.3
Analysis-Synthesis	19-D	8-1	7-1	10-0	58/90	16	85 (80-89)	2.8
Decision Speed	34	13-7	11-8	16-5	95/90	66	106 (101-111)	8.4
Memory for Words	18	17-6	12-1	>23	96/90	67	107 (99-114)	10.4
Rapid Picture Naming	106	10-6	9-3	12-1	73/90	34	94 (92-96)	5.7
Planning	-	10-11	4-7	>28	89/90	43	97 (86-109)	6.0
Pair Cancellation	67	>19	15-0	>19	99/90	92	121 (119-124)	12.8

Note. Norms based on age 12-3.

STEP-BY-STEP INTERPRETATION OF THE WJ III COG

The following section outlines a systematic way to evaluate an individual's performance on the WJ III COG. It includes six steps for interpretation. The first step involves consideration of the GIA scores. The second step emphasizes an analysis of strengths and weaknesses among cluster scores, especially the CHC factor scores. The third step provides a mechanism for determining whether there are significant differences between or among tests that comprise a cluster. Step four discusses how to determine if there are any practical implications of test score performance. The fifth step introduces a criterion-referenced interpretation schema that includes a link to performance predictions with cognitive tasks similar to those measured by the WJ III. The final step deals with consideration of variables that facilitate or inhibit cognitive performance, whether on the WJ III or in real life.

Step 1

Consider the GIA and interpret as needed. Determine whether an overall intelligence score is needed. Not all examiners use an overall or composite score, and some professionals do not believe that general intellectual ability is a useful construct, therefore, calculation of the GIA score is made by election in the WJ III CPP. To include the GIA, check "Include GIA/BIA Scores" as one of the score report options. If elected, the GIA age- or grade-equivalent, developmental zone, relative proficiency index, percentile rank, and standard scores will appear as a line on the Table of Scores. (Typically, the standard score and associated confidence band are the preferred metrics for interpretation of an intellectual ability score.)

DON'T FORGET

Remember to check "Include GIA/ BIA Scores" on the Score Report Options if you want them included in the Table of Scores and Summary narrative.

Step 2

Evaluate differences among cluster scores. Although general intellectual ability is "the single most important source of the school population's variance in test scores and scholastic achievement levels" (Jensen, 2000), its relevance for academic intervention is limited. In contrast, tests of distinct intellectual abilities, or those that deal with categorically defined kinds of tasks, can be more diagnostic. The WJ III COG Standard Battery includes cluster scores for three categories of intellectual abilities: Verbal Ability, Thinking Abilities, and Cognitive Efficiency. These cluster scores can be evaluated in the standard battery intracognitive discrepancy procedure. The WJ III COG Extended Battery includes the CHC factors (Comprehension-Knowledge, Long-Term Retrieval, Visual-Spatial Thinking, Auditory Processing, Fluid Reasoning, Processing Speed, and Short-Term Memory) as well as two other categories of special intellectual abilities (Phonemic Awareness and Working Memory) that can be evaluated in the extended battery intracognitive discrepancy procedure.

The intracognitive discrepancy procedure is based on the practice of examining test performance to determine patterns of strengths and weaknesses. This type of analysis is consistent with Brackett and McPherson's (1996) suggestion that "[a] major value of detecting severe discrepancies within and between areas of cognition is the focus on cognitive processing components of learning disabilities" (p. 79). Because the procedure makes it possible to identify a relative cognitive processing delay as early as first grade, it may be particularly useful for early identification of a learning difficulty.

In each of the intracognitive discrepancy options, the tests that comprise each interpretive cluster must be administered to obtain intracognitive discrepancies. In the WJ III CPP, each broad CHC ability standard score is compared to the average of all the other cognitive ability standard scores included in the comparison. The procedure can be used with either the standard or extended battery. Rapid Reference 4.3 outlines the clusters that are included in the intracognitive discrepancy procedure when using either battery.

Intracognitive discrepancies form a basis for determining whether information-processing strengths and weaknesses exist. Table 4.3 shows how an individual's cognitive abilities are analyzed in the intracognitive discrepancies section of the WJ III CPP Table of Scores. This example uses the set of seven broad CHC factors measured by the WJ III COG Extended Battery as well as two additional clusters: Phonemic Awareness and Working Memory. (The Phonemic Awareness and Working Memory clusters do not need to be administered to calculate intracognitive discrepancies. However, Phonemic Awareness can be included if Test 8: Incomplete Words is administered; Working Memory can be

≡Rapid Reference 4.3

WJ III Intracognitive Discrepancies

Standard	**Extended**
Verbal Ability	Comprehension-Knowledge (Gc)
Thinking Ability	Long-Term Retrieval (Glr)
Cognitive Efficiency	Visual-Spatial Thinking (Gv)
	Auditory Processing (Ga)
	Fluid Reasoning (Gf)
	Processing Speed (Gs)
	Short-Term Memory (Gsm)
	{Phonemic Awareness}[a]
	{Working Memory}[b]

[a]Phonemic Awareness is not required for calculation of intracognitive discrepancies. The Phonemic Awareness score is not included in the "Other" score calculated for the other clusters. The Phonemic Awareness score is compared to the same "Other" score as Auditory Processing (Ga).

[b]Working Memory is not required for calculation of intracognitive discrepancies. The Working Memory score is not included in the "Other" score calculated for the other clusters. The Working Memory score is compared to the same "Other" score as Short-Term Memory (Gsm).

Source: Adapted from *WJ III Technical Manual*, p. 6, Riverside Publishing 2001.

included if Test 9: Auditory Working Memory is administered.) After each factor or cluster name, the actual standard score obtained by the individual is listed. Next, the individual's predicted standard score is listed. (The predicted score is obtained from a regression equation.) The predicted score is compared to the actual score, and the difference is listed in the "Difference" column.

Two scores can help you interpret the presence and severity of any discrepancies: the *discrepancy percentile rank* (DISCREPANCY PR) and the *discrepancy standard deviation* (DISCREPANCY SD). The DISCREPANCY PR reflects the percent of the population that possesses a discrepancy of that magnitude, such as 5% or 7%. The DISCREPANCY SD is a standardized z score that changes the same discrepancy into standard deviation units, such as a criterion of ±1.5 standard deviations.

On the last column of Table 4.3 is a Yes/No list. For each cluster that meets the criterion for a significant discrepancy, a Yes is indicated. A No is indicated

Table 4.3 Compuscore Version 1.1b Score Report for Kayla W. (Intracognitive Discrepancies)

| DISCREPANCIES | STANDARD SCORES | | | DISCREPANCY | | Significant at |
	Actual	Predicted	Difference	PR	SD	+ or − 1.50 SD (SEE)
Intra-Cognitive						
COMP-KNOWLEDGE (Gc)	82	95	−13	15	−1.03	No
L-T RETRIEVAL (Glr)	75	95	−20	5	−1.67	Yes
VIS-SPATIAL THINK (Gv)	97	94	+3	59	+0.22	No
AUDITORY PROCESS (Ga)	107	92	+15	86	+1.10	No
FLUID REASONING (Gf)	77	95	−18	7	−1.51	Yes
PROCESS SPEED (Gs)	103	93	+10	76	+0.69	No
SHORT-TERM MEM (Gsm)	104	92	+12	82	+0.93	No
PHONEMIC AWARE	104	92	+12	80	+0.85	No
WORKING MEMORY	96	92	+4	62	+0.30	No

for each cluster that does not meet the criterion for a severe discrepancy. The criterion for significance is entered in the WJ III CPP. Available options range from ±2.3 to ±1.3 SD (or 1 to 10 percent of the population to be identified as possessing a severe discrepancy).

In the example provided, Long-Term Retrieval would meet the designated criterion (−1.5 SD) for a significant weakness. The individual's DISCREP-ANCY SD is −1.67. This means that the individual's actual Long-Term Retrieval score is 1.67 discrepancy standard deviation units lower than his or her predicted Long-Term Retrieval score. Fluid Reasoning would also meet the designated criterion for a significant weakness.

An important observation in the calculation of discrepancy norms is that the standard deviation of ability-achievement discrepancy scores is not 15. Frequently, professionals in the field calculate discrepancies between scores from ability and achievement tests that are on the standard score scale with a mean of 100 and standard deviation of 15. The erroneous assumption is then often made that the resulting discrepancy score is on the same scale.

Examiners may correctly assume that discrepancies of 1 or 1.5 standard deviations may be significant. This assumption is often erroneously translated to mean discrepancies of 15 (1 SD) or 22 (1.5 SD) standard score points. The error in this assumption is that discrepancy scores never have a standard deviation of 15. In the calculation of the WJ III Discrepancy Norms, typical ability-achievement standard deviations varied from 8 to 12 points. Thus, an ability-achievement standard score discrepancy of 8 to 12 points (depending on the curriculum area and the age or grade) actually represents a discrepancy that is 1 standard deviation above or below the mean discrepancy score. The ability-achievement standard deviations used to evaluate the significance of a discrepancy in the WJ III are the norm-based standard deviations (called the standard error of estimate) of the discrepancy distribution.

If you use the WJ III COG and the WJ III ACH together, an additional discrepancy procedure, called the intra-individual discrepancy procedures, is available for diagnosis and instructional planning. Like the intracognitive discrepancy procedure, the intra-individual discrepancy procedure is based on the practice of examining test performance to determine patterns of strengths and weaknesses. It differs from the intracognitive discrepancy procedure in that both cognitive and achievement measures are included in the analysis.

The intra-individual discrepancy procedure is an alternative to the traditional ability-achievement discrepancy model for establishing the presence of a learning disability. It can be used to identify a learning disability in lieu of, or in the absence of, an ability-achievement discrepancy. It can also be used to corroborate a diagnosis made on the basis of an ability-achievement discrepancy.

The intra-individual discrepancy procedure allows you to analyze an individual's cognitive and academic scores across the clusters of the WJ III COG and WJ III ACH and to explore co-varying cognitive and achievement strengths and weaknesses. Each cognitive ability and achievement area of interest is compared to the average of all other abilities in the comparison. This analysis is particularly useful in the identification of a specific learning disability when you need to determine the specific nature of the problem. The intra-individual discrepancy procedure is similar to the approach recommended by Fletcher et al. (1998), who advocated that examiners evaluate domain-specific achievement skills conjointly with related cognitive abilities. The procedure can be used with several combinations of clusters from the WJ III COG and WJ III ACH. Rapid Reference 4.4 includes four sets of tests that may be used in calculating intra-individual discrepancies. In each of the four options, the tests that comprise the interpretive cluster must be administered to obtain intra-individual discrepancies from the WJ III CPP.

The intra-individual discrepancy analysis can help you determine and document both strengths and weaknesses in learning abilities, as well as define how these abilities are related to the learning difficulties. For example, a reading problem may be caused by some underlying condition (such as poor phonological awareness or poor memory) that may affect others areas as well (e.g., memorization of math facts). As noted by Scarborough (1991), cognitive and achievement weaknesses can be viewed as "successive, observable symptoms of the same condition" (p. 38–39). Table 4.4 shows how these abilities are analyzed together in the Intra-Individual Discrepancies section of the WJ III CPP. This example uses the set of clusters from the extended cognitive and achievement batteries.

The intra-individual discrepancy procedure is most appropriate when the purposes of the assessment are to determine why the student has had academic difficulties, to explain how the difficulties relate to cognitive strengths and weaknesses, and to select appropriate interventions. This procedure is in line with current conceptualizations of multiple intelligences that specify that dif-

Rapid Reference 4.4

WJ III Intra-Individual Discrepancies

Intra-Individual Discrepancies

Standard ACH/Standard COG
Verbal Ability
Thinking Ability
Cognitive Efficiency
Broad Reading
Broad Math
Broad Written Language
Oral Language–Std

Extended ACH/Standard COG
Verbal Ability
Thinking Ability
Cognitive Efficiency
Basic Reading Skills
Reading Comprehension
Math Calculation Skills
Math Reasoning
Basic Writing Skills
Written Expression
Oral Expression
Listening Comprehension
Academic Knowledge

Standard ACH/Extended COG
Comprehension-Knowledge (Gc)
Long-Term Retrieval (Glr)
Visual Spatial-Thinking (Gv)
Auditory Processing (Ga)
Fluid Reasoning (Gf)
Processing Speed (Gs)
Short-Term Memory (Gsm)
{Phonemic Awareness}[a]
{Working Memory}[b]
Broad Reading
Broad Math
Broad Written Language
Oral Language–Std

Extended ACH/Extended COG
Comprehension-Knowledge (Gc)
Long-Term Retrieval (Glr)
Visual Spatial-Thinking (Gv)
Auditory Processing (Ga)
Fluid Reasoning (Gf)
Processing Speed (Gs)
Short-Term Memory (Gsm)
{Phonemic Awareness}[a]
{Working Memory}[b]
Basic Reading Skills
Reading Comprehension
Math Calculation Skills
Math Reasoning
Basic Writing Skills
Written Expression
Oral Expression
Listening Comprehension
Academic Knowledge

[a]Phonemic Awareness is not required for calculation of intra-individual discrepancies. The Phonemic Awareness score is not included in the "Other" score calculated for the other clusters. The Phonemic Awareness score is compared to the same "Other" score as Auditory Processing (Ga).

[b]Working Memory is not required for calculation of intra-individual discrepancies. The Working Memory score is not included in the "Other" score calculated for the other clusters. The Working Memory score is compared to the same "Other" score as Short-Term Memory (Gsm).

Source: Adapted from *WJ III Technical Manual*, p. 5, Riverside Publishing 2001.

Table 4.4 Compuscore Version 1.1b Score Report for Kayla W. (Intra-Individual Discrepancies)

DISCREPANCIES	STANDARD SCORES			DISCREPANCY		Significant at
	Actual	Predicted	Difference	PR	SD	+ or – 1.50 SD (SEE)
Intra-Individual						
COMP-KNOWLEDGE (Gc)	78	82	–4	33	–0.43	No
L-T RETRIEVAL (Glr)	67	86	–19	5	–1.60	Yes
VIS-SPATIAL THINK (Gv)	96	90	+6	65	+0.38	No
AUDITORY PROCESS (Ga)	104	87	+17	89	+1.23	No
FLUID REASONING (Gf)	67	85	–18	7	–1.51	Yes
PROCESS SPEED (Gs)	97	89	+8	73	+0.62	No
SHORT-TERM MEM (Gsm)	101	86	+15	90	+1.28	No
PHONEMIC AWARE	101	87	+14	87	+1.11	No
WORKING MEMORY	92	85	+7	73	+0.62	No
BASIC READING SKILLS	92	81	+11	89	+1.22	No
READING COMP	78	84	–6	22	–0.76	No
MATH CALC SKILLS	73	87	–14	11	–1.22	No
MATH REASONING	68	85	–17	3	–1.86	Yes
BASIC WRITING SKILLS	80	84	–4	34	–0.41	No
WRITTEN EXPRESSION	97	83	+14	90	+1.29	No
ORAL EXPRESSION	78	85	–7	26	–0.65	No
LISTENING COMP	91	82	+9	77	+0.75	No
ACADEMIC KNOWLEDGE	76	84	–8	20	–0.85	No

ferent cognitive processing capacities are related to solving different types of problems (Fletcher et al., 1998). For example, using this discrepancy procedure could help you detect a pattern of cognitive/linguistic weaknesses that are reflected in an individual's listening comprehension, reading comprehension, and written expression. At the same time, a pattern of strengths may be noted in fluid reasoning, math calculation, and math reasoning. In addition, the intra-individual discrepancy procedure can be used to identify a learning disability early on, rather than waiting until a child has failed in school for several years.

Step 3

Determine whether significant differences exist between or among the tests that comprise a cluster. The WJ III emphasizes the principle of cluster interpretation. However, when performance on two tests that comprise a cluster is significantly different, the cluster score may not adequately capture important interpretive information because each test in the cluster is intended to measure a qualitatively different narrow ability. Consequently, when tests that comprise a cluster differ significantly, you should interpret the individual's performance at the narrow ability (Stratum I) level.

To determine if there are significant differences between two tests that comprise a cluster, compare the confidence bands for the tests on the Standard Score/Percentile Rank Profile. The Standard Score/Percentile Rank Profile can be printed from the WJ III CPP. Figure 4.5 is a display from the Standard Score/Percentile Rank Profile. This profile portrays the 68% confidence band for an individual's standard scores and percentile ranks. The band provides a range of scores that would contain the point at which an individual's true score would fall two out of three times. The confidence band is centered on the individual's obtained score.

Rapid Reference 4.5 provides three rules for interpreting the differences between two tests in a cluster. When this procedure is applied to a cluster that is comprised of more than two tests (such as Broad Attention, Executive Processes, Cognitive Fluency, Thinking Ability–Std, Thinking Ability–Ext, Cognitive Efficiency–Ext, Brief Intellectual Ability, GIA-Std, GIA-Ext), multiple comparisons are being made, and it is possible that differences could be found as a result of chance. Consequently, the rules in the procedure are primarily

Peer Comparisons

-1 SEM   +1 SEM   Confidence
          68%   Band

Norms based on: Grade (K.0-12.9)

LONG-TERM
RETRIEVAL (Glr)

SS <40   40   50   60   70   80   90   100   110   120   130   140   150   160   >160
PR <0.1   0.1 0.5 1 2 5 7 10 15 20 30 40 50 60 70 80 85 90 93 95 98 99 99.5 99.9 >99.9

Visual-Auditory Learning

SS <40   40   50   60   70   80   90   100   110   120   130   140   150   160   >160
PR <0.1   0.1 0.5 1 2 5 7 10 15 20 30 40 50 60 70 80 85 90 93 95 98 99 99.5 99.9 >99.9

Retrieval Fluency

SS <40   40   50   60   70   80   90   100   110   120   130   140   150   160   >160
PR <0.1   0.1 0.5 1 2 5 7 10 15 20 30 40 50 60 70 80 85 90 93 95 98 99 99.5 99.9 >99.9

Figure 4.5 Portion of a Standard Score/Percentile Rank Profile

Rapid Reference 4.5

Rules for Interpreting Significant Difference Between Two Tests

1. If the confidence bands for any two tests or clusters overlap at all, assume that no statistically significant difference exists between the subject's true scores for these abilities.

2. If a separation exists between the ends of two test bands that is less than the width of the wider of the two bands, assume that a possible significant difference exists between the subject's true scores for these abilities.

3. If the separation between the two bands is greater than the width of the widest band, assume that a statistically significant difference exists between the subject's true scores for these abilities.

recommended for two-test comparisons. (You may want to determine if two unrelated tests or clusters are significantly different—for example, when all clusters have not been administered for calculation of intracognitive discrepancies.)

Interpretation of significant differences between tests or clusters should be made cautiously. A difference may be statistically significant, as determined by the Standard Score/Percentile Rank Profile, but the difference may not have any practical significance. The Age/Grade Profile is a better tool for determining the practical implications of differences in test or cluster performance.

Step 4

Determine whether there are any practical implications of cluster or test score performance. For each test administered, the WJ III CPP calculates a *developmental zone* that suggests the age (or grade) that the individual will find similar tasks easy and the age (or grade) at which the individual will find similar tasks difficult. The developmental zone is similar to Betts's (1957) independent and frustration levels and Vygotsky's zones of proximal development (Wertsch, 1985). The WJ III developmental zone extends Betts's conceptualization into the area of cognitive functioning. The WJ III developmental zone may closely parallel Vygotsky's conceptualization of a range that spans the distance between an individual's independent problem-solving ability and his or her ability when demonstrated through collaboration with adult guidance or more capable peers.

The WJ III developmental zone (defined as EASY to DIFF on the WJ III CPP) predicts an individual's proficiency with tasks along an age or grade scale. The lower point of the zone is the point at which the individual will find tasks quite easy and establishes a point at which he or she can perform the defined cognitive functions independently. The upper limit of the zone establishes the point at which the individual will find similar cognitive tasks difficult to perform without a great deal of help and motivation. In Vygotskian terms, the DIFF level is the point at which the individual may be capable of performing if provided collaboration with an adult mentor or more capable peer.

A practical application of the WJ III developmental zone is the Age/Grade Profile. These profiles can be printed from the WJ III CPP. Figure 4.6 shows a portion of an individual's Age/Grade Profile. For each ability plotted, the mid-point of the band represents the individual's age- or grade-equivalent score. The band extends downward on the age or grade scale to define a point at which the individual will find similar tasks easy, and it extends upward on the same scale to a point at which the individual will find similar tasks difficult. This graphic presentation can also be useful in conveying test results to parents or teachers. It helps illustrate the idea that individuals do not operate solely at a discrete age or grade point, but rather across a defined range of ability. For many cognitive abilities, that range can be quite wide. Note that the Age/Grade Profile also reports percentile ranks and RPIs. As a result, all of the important quantitative information about a subject's test performance is included in a single display.

Observe the developmental band for every cognitive test and cluster, and compare the band to the vertical line representing the individual's chronological age or current grade placement. If the vertical line falls to the right of the developmental zone, similar cognitive tasks, when presented at the individual's age or grade level, will be too difficult for him or her. Conversely, if the vertical line falls to the left of the developmental zone, similar cognitive tasks, when presented at the individual's age- or grade-level, will be very easy for him or her. For example, Figure 4.6 shows that knowledge, visual-spatial thinking, auditory processing, and fluid reasoning tasks will be too difficult for this individual if they are presented at his or her grade level (1.9).

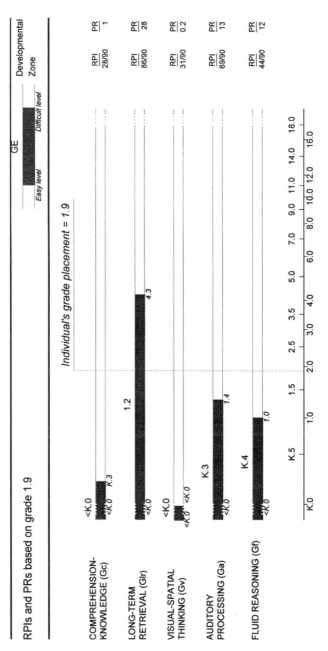

Figure 4.6 Portion of the Age/Grade Profile

Step 5

Use a criterion-referenced nomenclature to describe test performance and predict near-term performance with similar types of tasks. Although the WJ III is a norm-referenced battery of tests, the RPI makes possible criterion-referenced interpretations of test performance. These interpretations are accomplished when RPI scores are transformed into a nomenclature that provides a description of the quality of the performance. The nomenclature may be particularly useful for describing the presence and severity of any functional limitations, developmental delay, or cognitive impairment. (Other interpretive schemes use standard scores or percentile ranks as a basis for describing performance; however, those scores are more appropriately used to describe relative standing in a group, not quality of performance.) Rapid Reference 4.6 is an outline that suggests how to use the RPI score to provide a criterion-referenced description of task performance. The column labeled "Proficiency Level" allows you to describe any limitations the individual exhibited in task performance. The column labeled "Level of Development" may be particularly useful for assessing young children who have a delay in one or more aspects of cognitive development. The third column, labeled "Functional Level," may be appropriate for reporting levels of impairment or preserved function in clinical or neuropsychological assessment.

The RPI also enables you to make predictive statements about an individual's competency with similar tasks in reference to an age or grade comparison group. For example, if an individual obtained an RPI of 80/90 on Long-Term

≡ Rapid Reference 4.6

Criterion-Referenced Interpretation of RPI Scores

RPI	Proficiency Level	Developmental Level	Functional Level
97/90 to 100/90	Advanced	Advanced	Advanced
75/90 to 96/90	Average	Age-Appropriate	Within Normal Limits
25/90 to 74/90	Limited	Mildly Delayed	Mildly Impaired
4/90 to 24/90	Very Limited	Moderately Delayed	Moderately Impaired
0/90 to 3/90	Negligible	Extremely Delayed	Severely Impaired

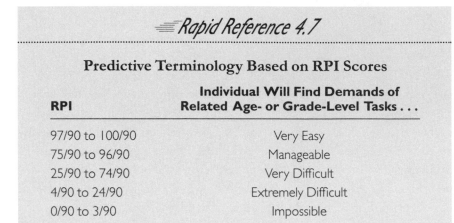

≋Rapid Reference 4.7

Predictive Terminology Based on RPI Scores

RPI	Individual Will Find Demands of Related Age- or Grade-Level Tasks . . .
97/90 to 100/90	Very Easy
75/90 to 96/90	Manageable
25/90 to 74/90	Very Difficult
4/90 to 24/90	Extremely Difficult
0/90 to 3/90	Impossible

Retrieval, you would predict that the individual would be able to manage age- or grade-level tasks that require the ability to store information and fluently retrieve it later through association. If the individual also obtained an RPI of 66/90 on Test 2: Visual-Auditory Learning, you would expect that this individual would have a very difficult experience learning similar paired-associate type age- or grade-level tasks. (Some examples of paired-associate tasks include learning the letters of the alphabet in Kindergarten or first grade or memorizing math facts in second or third grade.) Similarly, a RPI of 19/90 on Fluid Reasoning would enable you to predict extreme difficulty with age- or grade-level tasks involving a grasp of abstract concepts, generalizing rules, and seeing implications. For example, the individual may have extreme difficulty changing strategies if his or her first approach does not work. Rapid Reference 4.7 can be used to develop predictive statements from an individual's RPI score. Some possible implications of limitations, delay, or impairment on any of the WJ III COG clusters are provided in Rapid Reference 4.8.

Step 6

Consider the variables that may facilitate or inhibit the individual's cognitive or academic performance. External factors can influence test performance, just as noncognitive internal factors can. In the cognitive performance model presented earlier in this chapter, these factors were labeled "Facilitator-Inhibitors." These factors should be considered when interpreting an individual's performance on the

≡Rapid Reference 4.8

Possible Implications of Limitations, Delay, or Impairments

WJ III Cluster	Sample Implications of Limitations, Delay, or Impairments
Verbal Ability	Lack of information or language skills, or inability to communicate one's knowledge
Thinking Ability	Poor ability to use thinking processes when information cannot be processed automatically
Cognitive Efficiency	Difficulty in automatic cognitive processing
Comprehension-Knowledge (Gc)	Lack of information or language skills, or inability to communicate one's knowledge
Long-Term Retrieval (Glr)	Difficulty in recalling relevant information and in learning and retrieving previously stored knowledge; needs more repetition to learn than most peers; inconsistent in remembering previously learned material
Visual-Spatial Thinking (Gv)	Poor spatial orientation; misperception of object-space relationships; problems remembering visually presented material; tendency to miss subtle visual social and interpersonal cues
Auditory Processing (Ga)	Speech discrimination problems; poor phonological knowledge; failure in recognizing sounds; inability to distinguish speech sounds amid other noises; increased likelihood of misunderstanding complex verbal instructions
Fluid Reasoning (Gf)	Difficulty in grasping abstract concepts, generalizing rules, and seeing implications; may have difficulty changing strategies if first approach does not work
Short-Term Memory (Gsm)	Difficulty in remembering just-imparted instructions or information; easily overwhelmed by complex or multistep verbal directions
Processing Speed (Gs)	Slow in execution of easy cognitive tasks; slow acquisition of new material; tendency to become overwhelmed by complex events; need for extra time in responding even to well-practiced tasks; may have difficulty making correct conceptual decisions quickly
Cognitive Fluency	Slow in rate of cognitive task performance; slow in immediate recall of previously stored knowledge, general verbal information; slow in concept processing

(continued)

Phonological Awareness	Difficulty in discrimination of speech sounds; possible delay in literacy development or reading problems
Executive Processes	Poor problem-solving skills, self-regulation, inhibitory control, planning, and self-monitoring
Broad Attention	Poor cognitive control of more and more types of attentional functions
Working Memory	Difficulty with performing complex mental operations on material placed in short-term memory
Delayed Recall	Difficulty with remembering information that was learned previously; need for more repetition in learning

WJ III COG. The facilitator-inhibitors may have influenced test performance for better or worse, and outside the testing situation, they can often override the effects of cognitive strengths or weaknesses identified in the WJ III COG.

Organic integrity, motivation, attention, and personality or style variables are examples of internal facilitators or inhibitors. Organic integrity is an internal factor referring to overall health, intactness, and other physical aspects that impact the functioning of the sensory and central nervous systems. These aspects range from poor visual and auditory acuity to degenerative effects on the nervous system from conditions such as Alzheimer's disease or alcohol abuse. Motivation and attention variables are individual characteristics that influence attention and concentration (Hidi, 1990; Snow, 1989b). They are often task-specific but may vary from time to time for a given task. Significant motivation/attention variables include attention deficits, anxiety, interests, and the need for achievement. Personality and style variables represent the longer-term, often modifiable, characteristics of an individual that can be observed in the strategies and nature of an individual's problem-solving behavior. One example is reflection-impulsivity, an individual's tendency to respond carefully and accurately or to respond rapidly, but less accurately. Another example of a style variable is the tendency toward divergent versus convergent thinking.

External facilitator-inhibitors frequently operate in a given situation such as a particular physical setting or when a certain test is being used. The treatment component of an aptitude-treatment interaction research design (Snow, 1989a) is an example of an external facilitator-inhibitor. In a classroom situation, the physical environment and instructional methods are facilitator-inhibitors. The individual's home environment, including the stability of the family unit, is an important external factor.

Information on characteristics or conditions that both facilitate and inhibit performance can be gathered with other norm-referenced tests and informal measures, such as interviews, observations, and checklists. One example is the "Test Session Observations Checklist," located on each Test Record. This checklist is a brief, seven-category behavior rating scale intended to systematize and document a number of relevant examiner observations. The categories include levels of conversational proficiency, cooperation, and activity; attention and concentration; self-confidence; care in responding; and response to difficult tasks. A wide range of possible responses is provided for each category. Figure 4.7 is an example of a completed Test Session Observation Checklist.

This checklist should be used immediately after test administration. For each item, place a check mark in the box corresponding to the best description of the behavior that was observed as an individual was assessed; check only one category for each item. If any item does not apply to the individual, or if the categories do not convey an adequate description of the individual's test session behaviors, leave the item blank. Always make notes of any other behaviors that are of clinical interest.

If a school-aged child is being assessed, the child's classroom teacher can be an invaluable source of information on the facilitators and inhibitors. For example, teachers can contribute their observations of the student's temperament and typical mood. In addition to providing work samples for analysis, teachers can convey important information about the student's classroom performance, learning needs, and style. This information may include the amount of one-on-one attention required, average amount of schoolwork completed, follow-through on homework, attention to details in schoolwork, and ability to sustain attention long enough to complete grade-level tasks. For example, how does the student typically respond to tasks that require sustained mental effort? Listening ability, organization and orderliness, and ability to remember what he or she is supposed to do are important pieces of information that can be provided by the teacher. It is also important to learn the grade level at which the student is being instructed, because the level of instruction may be too easy or too difficult. If the student has a problem with attention or hyperactivity, information should be gathered from the teacher about his or her activity level both inside and outside of the classroom. The presence and severity of any

TEST SESSION OBSERVATIONS CHECKLIST

Check only one category for each item.

Level of conversational proficiency
- ☐ 1. Very advanced
- ☐ 2. Advanced
- ☑ 3. Typical for age/grade
- ☐ 4. Limited
- ☐ 5. Very limited

Level of cooperation
- ☐ 1. Exceptionally cooperative throughout the examination
- ☑ 2. Cooperative (typical for age/grade)
- ☐ 3. Uncooperative at times
- ☐ 4. Uncooperative throughout the examination

Level of activity
- ☐ 1. Seemed lethargic
- ☑ 2. Typical for age/grade
- ☐ 3. Appeared fidgety or restless at times
- ☐ 4. Overly active for age/grade; resulted in difficulty attending to tasks

Attention and concentration
- ☐ 1. Unusually absorbed by the tasks
- ☑ 2. Attentive to the tasks (typical for age/grade)
- ☐ 3. Distracted often
- ☐ 4. Consistently inattentive and distracted

Self-confidence
- ☐ 1. Appeared confident and self-assured
- ☑ 2. Appeared at ease and comfortable (typical for age/grade)
- ☐ 3. Appeared tense or worried at times
- ☐ 4. Appeared overtly anxious

Care in responding
- ☐ 1. Very slow and hesitant in responding
- ☐ 2. Slow and careful in responding
- ☑ 3. Prompt but careful in responding (typical for age/grade)
- ☐ 4. At times responded too quickly
- ☐ 5. Impulsive and careless in responding

Response to difficult tasks
- ☐ 1. Noticeably increased level of effort for difficult tasks
- ☑ 2. Generally persisted with difficult tasks (typical for age/grade)
- ☐ 3. Attempted but gave up easily
- ☐ 4. Would not try difficult tasks at all

Although background noise did seem to interfere with her concentration at times.

Figure 4.7 Example of a Completed Test Session Observations Checklist

Source: Adapted from *WJ III Tests of Cognitive Abilities* Test Record, p. I, Riverside Publishing 2001.

problem behaviors exhibited in the classroom should be identified. Classroom observations can help you independently confirm any problem behaviors reported and ascertain their severity.

If the individual being assessed is a child, the parents are typically in a good position to provide information on the child's current home and health status. For example, with whom does the child live? How many other people live in the same home? Have there been any recent changes at home? What is the child's overall physical health? Has he or she ever sustained a head injury or had a serious illness? Has the child had a recent vision and/or hearing test? Does the child sleep well, and for how long? Parents can also provide invaluable information about the child's temperament and mood, attitude toward school, and behaviors at home. Information gathered from the parents on the child's birth, infancy, early childhood, preschool, and school history can help you document the attainment of developmental milestones and any medical conditions that may influence present performance. When did the student learn important preschool tasks such as counting, the alphabet, and interactive play? How difficult was his/her behavior to manage during the preschool years? A brief history of the school years can also provide important information. For example, has the student ever repeated a grade or received special educational services? If there are any languages other than English spoken in the home, you should obtain additional information from the parents. For example, if the child was not born in this country, how long has he or she been here? What language was first learned by the child? What is the primary language spoken by the child at home? What is the primary language spoken by each of the other members of the family who live in the home? What is the child's primary language in informal social situations?

Adolescents and adults can usually provide valuable information about the conditions that facilitate or inhibit their own performance. They can typically describe their current home and health status, especially in response to a well-constructed checklist or comprehensive clinical interview. Important clinical information to be gathered includes feelings about the self and others, feelings about school or work, and motivations and interests. Since personality and style variables are typically well-established by adolescence or young adulthood, many individuals of these ages will be able to accurately describe important facilitator-inhibitors that influence their cognitive performance, such as their ability to concentrate, attention to detail, follow-through, organizational style, and orderliness.

1. **In the WJ III COG, the scores that provide the most important information for analysis of within-individual variability are the**

   (a) general intellectual ability (GIA) scores.

   (b) broad CHC clusters.

   (c) age- and grade-equivalent scores.

   (d) narrow ability (test) scores.

2. **The WJ III GIA scores are**

   (a) a distillate of cognitive abilities.

   (b) an aggregate of the cognitive tests comprising the composite.

   (c) the same as a Full Scale IQ score.

   (d) automatically calculated by the WJ III CPP if the component tests have been administered.

3. **The test weights used to calculate the GIA scores vary by age.** True or False?

4. **The two narrow abilities that comprise the Processing Speed cluster are**

   (a) correct decision speed and perceptual speed.

   (b) speed of information processing and spatial scanning.

   (c) rate of test taking and perceptual speed.

   (d) perceptual speed and semantic processing speed.

5. **Which of the following is not included in the Thinking Ability cluster?**

   (a) Comprehension-Knowledge

   (b) Long-Term Retrieval

   (c) Visual-Spatial Thinking

   (d) Auditory Processing

6. **Which of the following is not included in the category of executive functions?**

   (a) working memory

   (b) attention

   (c) planning

   (d) processing speed

7. **An individual who is impulsive and has difficulties with sequencing might be expected to have difficulty with which one of these tests?**

   (a) Planning

   (b) Concept Formation

   (c) Spatial Relations

   (d) Sound Blending

8. **Age- and grade-equivalent scores are**
   (a) the preferred scores for test interpretation.
   (b) not standards of performance.
   (c) not useful interpretive scores.
   (d) only useful for school-aged individuals.

9. **Which of the following is not a score option on the WJ III CPP?**
   (a) CALP level
   (b) *T*-score
   (c) stanine
   (d) 99% confidence band

10. **The intracognitive discrepancy procedure is based on the practice of examining test performance to determine patterns of strengths and weaknesses.** True or False?

11. **Which scores help examiners interpret the presence and severity of any discrepancies?**
   (a) standard scores and percentile ranks
   (b) RPIs and standard scores
   (c) the discrepancy percentile rank and discrepancy standard deviation
   (d) *T*-scores and stanines

12. **To determine whether the scores for tests that comprise a cluster differ significantly from one another, the examiner should consult the**
   (a) Age/Grade Profile.
   (b) Standard Score/Percentile Rank Profile.
   (c) Compuscore and Profiles Program.
   (d) WJ III *Technical Manual.*

13. **A practical application of the developmental zone is the**
   (a) Confidence band.
   (b) RPI.
   (c) Age/Grade Profile.
   (d) Standard Score/Percentile Rank Profile.

14. **It is possible to use a criterion-referenced interpretation of WJ III COG performance.** True or False?

15. **Which of the following is not a source of information about facilitator-inhibitors?**
   (a) parents
   (b) teachers
   (c) observations
   (d) hypnotherapy

Answers: 1. b; 2. a; 3. True; 4. d; 5. a; 6. d; 7. a; 8. b; 9. d; 10. True; 11. c; 12. b; 13. c; 14. True; 15. d

Five

STRENGTHS AND WEAKNESSES OF THE WJ III COG

This chapter covers the most salient strengths and weaknesses of the WJ III COG, organized according to six criteria commonly used to evaluate psychological tests: (1) theory, (2) test content, (3) administration and scoring options, (4) interpretation features, (5) technical characteristics, and (6) quality of materials.

THEORY

The WJ III provides for adequate measurement of nine broad cognitive abilities defined by CHC theory. The WJ III COG measures Fluid Intelligence (*Gf*), Crystallized Intelligence (*Gc*), Visual-Spatial Thinking (*Gv*), Auditory Processing (*Ga*), Short-Term Memory (*Gsm*), Long-Term Storage and Retrieval (*Glr*), and Processing Speed (*Gs*). (Reading-Writing [*Grw*] and Quantitative Knowledge [*Gq*] are two broad abilities measured by the WJ III Tests of Achievement [WJ III ACH].) This theoretical basis allows decisions regarding test selection and test interpretation to be made within the context of the research on the relationship between cognitive abilities and academic achievement (Flanagan, Ortiz, Alfonso, & Mascolo, 2002). In addition, this research base informs the interpretation of the relationships between and among the broad and narrow cognitive abilities and the impact of these abilities and their relationships to one another on knowledge acquisition and new learning.

TEST CONTENT

The content of the WJ III COG was designed to improve on its predecessor's breadth and depth of coverage. Two or three qualitatively different indicators of *Gf, Gc, Gv, Ga, Gsm, Glr,* and *Gs* are included in each cognitive factor score.

These measures allow for a greater understanding of an individual's strengths and weaknesses in cognitive functioning. The battery also includes a number of *clinical clusters*, including Working Memory, Executive Processes, and Broad Attention. These clusters are broad and multifaceted and do not represent factorially pure constructs. Additional validation studies are necessary to more fully realize the utility of these clinical clusters.

ADMINISTRATION AND SCORING OPTIONS

The WJ III COG includes 20 tests. As would be expected with a battery of this size, considerable time is required to master the administration and scoring procedures. In order to maximize the interpretative information, scoring is done primarily by computer; there are limited options for hand scoring. Approximate AEs and GEs are available as the tests are administered. However, RPI, standard scores, percentile ranks, and computer-generated profiles are not available until the raw scores have been entered into the WJ III Compuscore and Profiles Program. This extra step may be a drawback for some examiners, particularly those who use standard scores and percentile ranks when providing information to teachers immediately upon completion of testing. Also, the vast number of options on the scoring program and the sheer number of scores presented may be daunting, especially to a novice WJ III examiner.

INTERPRETATION FEATURES

Among the major strengths of the WJ III is the wealth of interpretive options that it offers. For example, the WJ III provides actual norms for interpreting discrepancies. In addition, its interpretive framework integrates structural (i.e., psychometric) and information-processing models. Although the variety of its interpretive options may appear overwhelming to novice practitioners, experienced WJ III examiners recognize their utility.

TECHNICAL CHARACTERISTICS

The standardization sample of 8,818 individuals is large compared to similar instruments. The norming sample was selected based on key individual and community variables. Bias toward any specific type of community or group was avoided by applying 13 socioeconomic status variables during the selection process for communities. Oversampling of minorities was conducted to ensure adequate representation of these groups. Norms are reported by one-month intervals from age 2-0 to 18-11 and then by one-year intervals from 19-0 to 95+ years of age. Grade norms are reported for each 10th of a school year from grade K.0 to 18.0.

Reliability characteristics for the WJ III COG are quite good. Most test reliabilities are at .80 or higher. Most cluster reliabilities are .90 or higher.

The authors of the WJ III closely followed the construct validation concepts of Messick (1995, 1998) that now serve as the foundation for the validity standards in the joint *Standards for Educational and Psychological Testing* (AERA, APA, & NCME, 1999), resulting in adequate representation of the broad CHC abilities that comprise this instrument. In addition, the WJ III's underlying item-response theory (IRT) growth scale (Rasch-based *W*-scale) is beneficial for measuring growth and conducting longitudinal research. Also contributing to the overall technical quality of the WJ III is its use of continuous norms and provision of a unique standard error of measurement (SEM) at each level of ability. The WJ III *Technical Manual* contains extensive information about the validity of this instrument, including substantive (content), structural (factor analysis), and external (predictive) validity evidence.

QUALITY OF MATERIALS

The WJ III is lighter, smaller, and less cumbersome than its predecessor. In addition, the WJ III easels include icons (e.g., headphones, stopwatch) as reminders to examiners during administration, and its scoring templates are sturdier. An unfortunate side effect of producing a smaller easel was a reduction in the size of the print, which could pose a problem for some practitioners. In addition, like its predecessor, the WJ III does not include manipulatives, which many practitioners find useful for evaluating certain populations (e.g., preschoolers, culturally and linguistically diverse individuals).

The primary strengths and weaknesses of the WJ III COG are summarized in Rapid Reference 5.1.

Primary Strengths and Weaknesses of the WJ III COG

Primary strengths	Primary weaknesses
• The battery is based on a well-validated theory of cognitive abilities. • It offers valid information about cognitive strengths and weaknesses. • It was conormed with the WJ III Tests of Achievement and provides actual discrepancy norms. • The instrument is of high technical quality. • The test materials are of high quality.	• The battery is necessarily complex; considerable time is required for the study and mastery of administration and scoring. • The sheer number of interpretive options and features may be overwhelming to new examiners. • Lack of hand scoring—beyond that provided by estimated AEs and GEs—limits the ability to provide immediate feedback to teachers. • Additional validity evidence is necessary to realize the utility of the clinical clusters.

🐟 TEST YOURSELF 🐟

1. **The Cattell-Horn-Carroll theory of cognitive abilities provides a framework for interpretation of the WJ III COG.** True or False?

2. **Which of the following would *not* be considered a clinical cluster?**

    (a) Working Memory

    (b) Auditory Processing

    (c) Executive Processes

    (d) Broad Attention

3. **The reliabilities of the WJ III COG clusters are mostly**

    (a) .90 or above.

    (b) .80 or above.

    (c) .70 or above.

    (d) .60 or above.

4. **The WJ III construct validation concepts draw heavily from the work of Messick.** True or False?

5. **The WJ III COG is smaller and lighter than its predecessor.** True or False?

Answers: 1.True; 2. b; 3. a; 4.True; 5.True

Six

CLINICAL USE OF THE WJ III
DISCREPANCY PROCEDURES*

From a historical perspective, the development and subsequent revisions of the Woodcock-Johnson Psycho-Educational Battery (Woodcock & Johnson, 1977; Woodcock & Johnson, 1989; Woodcock, McGrew, & Mather, 2001) parallels the enactment and implementation of the federal Education of All Handicapped Children Act (EAHCA). In 1975, when the EAHCA was first enacted, many states reported problems with establishing objective criteria for identifying a learning disability. With the goal of establishing objective and accurate criteria for identifying children for services, the U.S. Office of Education adopted the criterion of an *ability-achievement discrepancy* between intellectual ability and achievement in an effort to operationalize a distinction between children with LD and those with other academic problems. The inclusion of this criterion represented an attempt to classify low-achieving students into two categories: those with unexpected low achievement and those with expected low achievement (or underachievers). From the outset, the concept of an ability-achievement discrepancy has been controversial, but as Lyon, Fletcher, Shaywitz, Shaywitz, Torgesen, Wood, Schulte, & Olson (2001) point out, the idea of using this type of discrepancy model was "probably reasonable at the time" (p. 266). That is, many people in the 1970s viewed IQ scores as predictors of ability to learn.

Today, conceptualizations of the presence and nature of specific learning disabilities are changing. As a reflection of some of the changing conceptualizations, the authors of the WJ III have developed several alternatives for determining the presence and severity of psycho-educational discrepancies. In the WJ III, there are two fundamentally different types of discrepancy proce-

*This chapter is based, in part, on the concepts previously articulated by Mather & Schrank (2001).

120

dures—ability/achievement discrepancy and intra-ability discrepancy procedures. Because the WJ III COG was co-normed with the WJ III Tests of Achievement (WJ III ACH), several discrepancy procedures are available to professionals who use both batteries together. This chapter describes the uses for each of these types of discrepancy procedures.

Regardless of the procedure, all discrepancy scores obtained from the WJ III are actual scores based on norms, not scores estimated from a subsequently obtained correlation between two separately normed tests. The WJ III discrepancies are based on direct comparisons of actual scores for the 8,000+ subjects in the norming sample. Because all norms for the WJ III COG and the WJ III ACH are based on data from the same sample, you utilize discrepancies between and among an individual's WJ III scores. You don't need to rely on estimated discrepancies. Estimated discrepancies, based on the simple regression model, do not control for unknown differences that exist when using two tests based on different norming samples (e.g., the difference between means which is not known but may be several standard deviation points). Additionally, the WJ III discrepancy procedures are more accurate as they are sensitive to population shifts in the relationships between predictor and criterion variables at each age and grade level. (See the *WJ III Technical Manual* [McGrew & Woodcock, 2001] for more detail about the preparation of the WJ III ability-achievement discrepancy norms.)

The WJ III Compuscore and Profiles Program (WJ III CPP; Schrank & Woodcock, 2001) allows you the choice of determining the criterion for determining if a discrepancy is significant. This is done by selecting "Options" from the WJ III CPP menu bar. The "Program Options" selection will appear; it should be selected. This will open the Program Options window. Select the "Report Options" tab. On the Report Options tab, you may make your selection for the "Discrepancy Cutoffs."

This selection is how you will define your criterion for the statistical significance of a reported discrepancy.

If your criterion for a significant discrepancy is expressed in terms of standard deviation units (such as −1.5 SD), you should pay particular attention to the first column when

DON'T FORGET
....
All discrepancies obtained from the WJ III are actual discrepancy scores based on norms, not discrepancy scores estimated from a correlation between separately normed measures.

making your selection. It is labeled "SD (SEE)." (*SEE* is the abbreviation for *standard error of the estimate*. The SEE is the standard deviation of the actual WJ III ACH scores around the predicted achievement score for the group of individuals who have the same ability score and are at the same age or grade.) Alternatively, if you wish to determine significance based on the percentage of the population to be identified as having an ability-achievement discrepancy or an intra-ability weakness, you should pay particular attention to the second column; it is labeled "Low PR." This column identifies the percentage of the population that would be identified as having a significant weakness or ability-achievement discrepancy. The column labeled "High PR" shows the percentage of the population that would have achievement scores *significantly higher* than ability scores in an ability-achievement discrepancy procedure. This column signifies the population-percentage cutoff for significant strengths in the intra-ability discrepancy procedures.

Rapid Reference 6.1 shows the relationship between the standard deviation cutoffs and the percentage of the population to be identified as having a discrepancy. Many educational agencies utilize a −1.5 SD cutoff for determining if a discrepancy is significant. Using this criteria, seven percent of the population would be identified as having an ability-achievement discrepancy or an intra-ability weakness. Another commonly utilized criterion is −1.75 SD; this cutoff would identify 4 percent of the population as having an ability-achievement discrepancy (or an intra-ability weakness).

The distribution of discrepancy scores is fairly normal. To exemplify, when using plus or minus 2 SD in an intra-ability discrepancy procedure, 2 percent of the population would be identified as having a significant weakness and another 2 percent of the population would be identified as having a significant strength. (On the WJ III CPP, the "High PR" cutoff of 98 suggests that 2 percent of the population would be identified as having a significant strength.) Many professionals do not realize that the same is true for ability-achievement discrepancies. That is, the WJ III normative data show that the same percentage of individuals will show an achievement-to-ability weakness as do those that show an achievement-to-ability strength. (These are individuals whose achievement exceeds their ability scores.)

Some professionals or educational agencies have adopted a more liberal cutoff for determining significance. Consequently, the *Report Writer for the WJ III* (Schrank & Woodcock, 2002) allows you to select a significance cutoff as

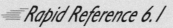

Rapid Reference 6.1

Discrepancy Cutoffs and Percentage of the Popoulation Identified as Having a Discrepancy

SD (SEE) Cutoff	Weakness	Strength
1.00	16%	16%
1.05	15%	15%
1.10	14%	14%
1.15	13%	13%
1.20	12%	12%
1.25	11%	11%
1.30	10%	10%
1.35	9%	9%
1.40	8%	8%
1.50	7%	7%
1.55	6%	6%
1.65	5%	5%
1.75	4%	4%
1.90	3%	3%
2.00	2%	2%
2.30	1%	1%

low as ±1 SD. This cutoff would identify 16 percent of the population as having an ability-achievement discrepancy. When this criterion is used in the intra-ability procedures, 16 percent of the population would be identified as having a significant weakness, and another 16 percent of the population would be identified as having a significant strength.

ABILITY-ACHIEVEMENT DISCREPANCY PROCEDURES

The WJ III ability-achievement discrepancy procedures are intended for use in predicting an individual's achievement from different mixes of ability tests. There are three ability-achievement discrepancy procedures on the WJ III.

These are called the Predicted Achievement/Achievement discrepancy procedure, the General Intellectual Ability/Achievement discrepancy procedure, and the Oral Language Ability/Achievement discrepancy procedure. The nature and purpose of each of these ability-achievement discrepancy procedures differs, as described below.

Predicted Achievement/Achievement Discrepancy Procedure

Among the ability-achievement discrepancy procedures available on the WJ III, the most accurate prediction of academic performance is obtained when using the Predicted Achievement/Achievement discrepancy procedure. This procedure was named to clearly convey its purpose—to predict an individual's academic performance based upon his or her levels of associated cognitive abilities. The name also differentiates this type of procedure from the WJ III General Intellectual Ability/Achievement and Oral Language Ability/Achievement procedures, as well as from other practices in which a global IQ score is used as a predictor.

The Predicted Achievement procedure is based on weighted combinations of Tests 1–7 of the WJ III COG. The test weights vary developmentally because the relationships among cognitive abilities and achievement areas also vary with age. For example, in the prediction of reading, the abilities most heavily weighted at grade 1 differ from the abilities most heavily weighted during the secondary school years. In the early grades, Test 4: Sound Blending is more heavily weighted than some other cognitive abilities, but, in the later school grades, Test 1: Verbal Comprehension is more heavily weighted. The weights reflect the relationships among the cognitive abilities when used as the best collective prediction of achievement areas. Each prediction is accomplished by statistically weighting the cognitive tasks from Tests 1–7 that are most associated with performance in a particular academic area.

The empirically defined relationships among the tests help predict the level at which the individual should be performing in each academic area, given his or her levels of associated cognitive abilities. (Statistically, this level is the mean achievement of others in the WJ III norming sample at the same age or grade and with the same cognitive scores.) A student with a cognitive weakness in an ability closely associated with mathematics, for example, will obtain a predicted mathematics score that reflects the weakness. That is, the student's mathematics achievement predicted score would be lower because others in the norming sample with that weakness scored lower. If the student shows a cognitive strength that is related to mathematics performance, his or her predicted mathematics score would be higher. If the

DON'T FORGET

The most accurate prediction of academic performance is obtained when using the WJ III Predicted Achievement/Achievement discrepancy procedure.

option is elected, predicted achievement scores for each academic area will be found in the Predicted Standard Score column in the "Predicted Achievement/Achievement Discrepancies" section in the Table of Scores when using one of the WJ III software programs.

The WJ III Predicted Achievement/Achievement discrepancy procedure can help document unexpected poor performance, but it should not be used as an estimate a student's potential for future school success. Rather, its purpose is to predict near-term academic functioning in each curricular area, based on others with the same current pattern of cognitive abilities. In other words, the intent of the Predicted Achievement/Achievement discrepancy procedure is to determine if the person is currently performing as well as one would expect, *given his or her levels of associated cognitive abilities* on Tests 1–7.

It is important to note that a student with a specific learning disability may, *or may* not, exhibit a Predicted Achievement/Achievement discrepancy. This is because the WJ III Predicted Achievement scores are highly predictive of the associated areas of academic achievement. Consequently, a weak cognitive ability or abilities may also attenuate the predicted achievement score. As stated by Flanagan, McGrew, and Ortiz (2000):

Specifically, the greater the predictive utility of the aptitude measure . . . the *less likely* a finding of significant ability-achievement discrepancy will be for an individual whose academic skill deficiencies cannot be explained by conative, environmental, instructional, or other (exclusionary) factors. This is counter to the inherent meaning of an ability-achievement discrepancy found in most federal and state definitions of (and criteria for identifying) learning disabilities—that is, a significant discrepancy indicates the presence of a learning disability and a nonsignificant discrepancy indicates the absence of a learning disability. (p. 383)

For example, a child with poor basic reading skills may obtain low scores on measures of auditory processing. Thus, the predicted achievement score for reading reflects this weakness, and the child may not show a discrepancy between predicted achievement and actual achievement. The predicted achievement cluster predicts that the child will struggle with reading, and he or she usually does.

When a significant discrepancy exists between predicted achievement and actual achievement, the observed difference suggests that the measured abilities related to the domain (e.g., vocabulary or phonological awareness) is not the factor or factors inhibiting performance. Other extrinsic factors (e.g., lack of proper instruction, economic disadvantage, lack of opportunity to learn, lack of interest, poor instruction, or poor motivation) may be causal or contributing factors. An observed Predicted Achievement/Achievement discrepancy should alert the examiner to consider extrinsic factors that may be contributing to poor academic performance, or other intrinsic factors such as narrow cognitive abilities that may be related to reading but that are not part of the predicted achievement score (e.g., rapid automatized naming).

General Intellectual Ability/Achievement Discrepancy Procedure

Despite early attempts by some leading theoreticians of the time to discourage the use of a global intellectual ability score as a measure of learning potential (Thorndike, 1963), the practice of using an IQ score as the ability measure in an ability-achievement discrepancy analysis became operationalized in 1977 at both the state policy level and at the practice level in the schools. Today, many state rules and regulations continue to include this criterion for LD eligibility. Consequently, the General Intellectual Ability/ Achievement discrepancy procedure was developed, in part, to address the language of federal legislation that posits "a severe discrepancy between achievement and intellectual ability," as part of the eligibility criteria for LD.

The WJ III General Intellectual Ability/Achievement discrepancy procedures were also designed to address some of the psychometric problems inherent in the ability-achievement discrepancy model. Because the WJ III COG and ACH are co-normed, you can be confident that any differences found between an individual's ability and achievement scores are not due to differences between two separate norm groups. Additionally, all WJ III discrepancy scores implicitly include the appropriate correction for regression to the mean, eliminating a source of systematic bias for individuals with ability scores above or below the mean. Computer scoring also enables you to obtain a distillate of general intellectual ability, or g, rather than using an equally-weighted composite score. The WJ III GIA scores are the first principal component (g) measures obtained from principal component analyses. Each GIA score (Standard and Extended) is a weighted combination of cognitive tests that accounts for the largest portion of variance in the component tests. The GIA score represents a common ability (g) underlying performance on all the tests used in the scale.

The General Intellectual Ability/Achievement discrepancy procedure uses a distillate first-principle component general intellectual ability (g) score as a global predictor across achievement domains, not an aggregate, equally-weighted full scale score (see Chapter 4). Although the intent of this discrepancy procedure is the same as the Predicted Achievement/Achievement discrepancy procedure—that is, to predict if the person is performing at the level of their cognitive abilities—the prediction is not domain specific. That is, separate prediction equations are not available for different academic areas.

In this procedure, either the General Intellectual Ability–Standard [GIA (Std)] or General Intellectual Ability–Extended [GIA (Ext)] score can be used as the ability measure. The GIA (Std) is derived from the first seven tests in the WJ III COG. Each of the seven tests represents a different CHC broad factor. The GIA (Ext) score is derived from the 14 tests that also provide the broad CHC factors. The WJ III Brief Intellectual Ability (BIA) score is not used for calculating ability-achievement discrepancies. That score is intended for screening purposes.

Oral Language Ability/Achievement Discrepancy Procedure

Among other problems inherent in the intellectual ability-achievement discrepancy model, there is no evidence that an observed discrepancy between intellectual ability and reading achievement helps describe any intrinsic reading-related processing problem (Torgesen, Wagner, Rashotte, Rose, Lindamood, Conway, & Garvan, 1999). Therefore, the intellectual ability-achievement discrepancy model does not diagnose a reading problem. In the areas of reading and writing disabilities, one traditional discrepancy model is to compare oral language abilities to reading and writing performance. This model was articulated by Woodcock (1956) in his doctoral dissertation:

> In the past few years there have been a number of techniques and tests developed which base expectancy of achievement upon some measure of oral language comprehension. The disparity between the oral comprehension level and reading achievement is assumed to be a relative indication of the prognosis of a remedial reading case. If the child is able to understand and use oral language at a level significantly higher than his ability to utilize written language this would be a favorable sign indicating room for improvement in the area of written language. It is known that children learn on the basis of past experience and it would appear that the child who has facility in oral language has a foundation for learning the printed symbols of written language. (p. 31)

The WJ III ACH contains an ability-achievement discrepancy procedure where the Oral Language-Extended cluster is used as the measure of ability. As noted by Stanovich (1991), use of an oral language measure to predict reading and writing is often preferable to use of a general intelligence score and is more in line with the concepts of *potential* and *unexpected failure*. A comparison of oral language ability to academic performance allows for a more circumscribed prescription of disability. Essentially, what distinguishes the individual with a reading disability from other poor readers is that listening comprehension is higher than reading comprehension (Rack, Snowling, & Olson, 1992), and thus the difficulty is "unpredicted." The relevant discrepancy is then a comparison of oral language ability, including listening comprehension and vocabulary, to reading comprehension. One important aspect of a learning disability evaluation is to distinguish between children whose problems are specific to one or more cognitive domains from those whose problems result from a more pervasive impairment in language skills (which may be more appropriately classified as an oral language disorder; Fletcher et al., 1998). Children who struggle in most aspects of language, as well as in many nonverbal domains, may be more appropriately classified as having some degree of mental impairment (e.g., mild to moderate mental retardation).

Using oral language ability as the aptitude measure moves us closer to a more principled definition of reading disability because it provides a more accurate estimate of what the person could achieve if the reading problem were entirely resolved. The Oral Language Ability/Achievement procedure has particular relevance for helping distinguish between individuals with adequate oral language capabilities, but poor reading and writing abilities (e.g., specific reading disability), versus individuals whose oral language abilities are commensurate with present levels of reading and writing performance. In the first case, when oral language performance is higher than reading ability, instructional recommendations would focus on reading and writing development. In the second case, instructional recommendations would be directed to all aspects of language development. A student with a learning disability may or may not exhibit an oral language ability/achievement discrepancy. For example, an older student with reading difficulties may have depressed performance in oral language because of his or her limited experiences with text. This lack of exposure to print contributes to reduced knowledge and vocabulary. The Oral Language Ability/Achievement discrepancy procedure is described in more detail in a companion volume entitled Essentials of WJ III Tests of Achievement Assessment (Mather, Wendling, & Woodcock, 2001).

INTRA-ABILITY DISCREPANCY PROCEDURES

The WJ III is well suited for analysis of test performance to determine patterns of strengths and weaknesses. This type of careful examination of test performance is recommended in the *Standards for Educational and Psychological Testing* (AERA, 1999):

DON'T FORGET

The Oral Language Ability/Achievement procedure has particular relevance for helping distinguish between individuals with adequate oral language capabilities, but poor reading and writing abilities (e.g., specific reading disability), versus individuals whose oral language abilities are commensurate with present levels of reading and writing performance.

Because each test in a battery examines a different function, ability, skill, or combination thereof, the test taker's performance can be understood best when scores are not combined or aggregated, but rather when each score is interpreted within the context of all other scores and assessment data. For example, low scores on timed tests alert the examiner to slowed responding as a problem that may not be apparent if scores on different kinds of tests are combined. (p. 123)

The WJ III intra-ability discrepancy procedures are intended for ipsative analysis of relative strengths and weaknesses in test performance. There are three intra-ability discrepancy procedures in the WJ III. These are called the Intracognitive, Intra-achievement and Intra-individual discrepancy procedures. The intra-ability discrepancies have a different purpose from the ability-achievement discrepancies, and they function differently. These discrepancy procedures are intended for diagnostic purposes, not predictive purposes. Instead of predicting an achievement score from an ability score, each ability is compared to the average of all of the other abilities in the comparison. This bi-directional comparison helps to determine patterns of relative strengths and weaknesses.

All of the WJ III discrepancy procedures of the WJ III reflect statistical rarity in score differences as compared to the general population (the discrepancy norms). When using the intra-ability discrepancy procedures, however, it is important to remember that an identified weakness is not necessarily serious enough to be classified as an impairment or a deficiency. (Impairments, limitations, or developmental delays can more adequately be described as a function of the Relative Proficiency Index, or RPI. See Chapter 4.) Indeed, some rarities are valuable deviations, and not all intra-ability weaknesses are abnormal in the negative sense. Differences between test scores may be statistically significant and rare, but they are not always or necessarily clinically meaningful. You should always seek to establish meaningful clinical significance as well as statistical significance. "The major weakness of the statistical rarity approach is that it has no values; it lacks any system for differentiating between desirable and un-

DON'T FORGET

The WJ III intra-ability discrepancy procedures are intended for ipsative analysis of relative strengths and weaknesses in test performance.

desirable behaviors. Of course, most users of the statistical rarity approach acknowledge that not all rarities should be identified as abnormal" (Alloy, Acocella, & Bootzin, 1996, p. 6).

Intracognitive Discrepancy Procedure

The WJ III COG includes an Intracognitive discrepancy procedure for analysis of an individual's relative cognitive strengths and weaknesses. Use of the Intracognitive discrepancy procedure is described in Chapter 4.

The intracognitive discrepancy procedure is in line with current conceptualizations of multiple intelligences, and the concept that individuals exhibit different patterns of strengths and weaknesses among cognitive abilities. The intracognitive discrepancy procedure is particularly useful in identifying *cognitive processing* or *information processing* strengths and weaknesses. Many states and school districts require documentation of a processing disorder for learning disabilities services. The intra-cognitive discrepancy procedure can be used for this purpose and is consistent with Brackett and McPherson's (1996) suggestion that "[a] major value of detecting severe discrepancies within and between areas of cognition is the focus on cognitive processing components of learning disabilities (p. 79)."

Clinicians have long understood the need to identify some sort of psychological dysfunction as an explanatory mechanism for deficient academic performance—yet there has been little if any theoretical specification to guide or support this practice; hence, the myriad of illogical assumptions that are often made (Flanagan et. al. 2002). The intracognitive discrepancy procedure can be thought of as representing an information-processing perspective that can include, in addition to the WJ III CHC factors, working memory and phonological awareness. Generally speaking, the abilities included in the intra-cognitive discrepancy procedure can provide information about an individual's levels of cognitive abilities that may impact his or her learning.

Rapid Reference 6.2 provides a summary of the recent literature on the relationship between cognitive abilities and specific academic achievements (Flanagan et al., 2002). For example, narrow abilities subsumed by Gc (lexical knowledge, language development, listening ability), Gsm (working memory), Ga (phonetic coding), Glr (naming facility), and Gs (perceptual speed) have been found to be related significantly to reading achievement. Similarly,

Rapid Reference 6.2

Relationships Between CHC Abilities and Academic Achievement

CHC Ability	Reading Achievement	Math Achievement	Writing Achievement
Gf	Inductive (I) and general sequential reasoning (RG) abilities play a moderate role in reading comprehension.	**Inductive (I) and general sequential (RG) reasoning abilities are consistently very important at all ages.**	Inductive (I) and general sequential reasoning abilities are related to basic writing skills primarily during the elementary school years (e.g., ages 6–13) and consistently related to written expression at all ages.
Gc	**Language development (LD), lexical knowledge (VL), and listening ability (LS) are important at all ages. These abilities become increasingly more important with age.**	**Language development (LD), lexical knowledge (VL), and listening abilities (LS) are important at all ages. These abilities become increasingly more important with age.**	**Language development (LD), lexical knowledge (VL), and general information (K0) are important primarily after age 7. These abilities become increasingly more important with age.**
Gsm	Memory span (MS) is important especially when evaluated **within the context of working memory.**	Memory span (MS) is important especially when evaluated **within the context of working memory.**	Memory span (MS) is important to writing, especially spelling skills whereas working memory has shown relationships with advanced writing skills (e.g., written expression).
Gv		May be important primarily for higher-level or advanced mathematics (e.g., geometry, calculus).	

Ga	Phonetic coding (PC) or "phonological awareness/processing" is very important during the elementary school years.	Phonetic coding (PC) or "phonological awareness/processing" is very important during the elementary school years for both basic writing skills and written expression (primarily before age 11).
Glr	Naming facility (NA) or "rapid automatic naming" is very important during the elementary school years. Associative memory (MA) may be somewhat important at select ages (e.g., age 6).	Naming facility (NA) or "rapid automatic naming" has demonstrated relationships with written expression, primarily the fluency aspect of writing.
Gs	Perceptual speed (P) abilities are important during all school years, particularly the elementary school years.	Perceptual speed (P) abilities are important during all school years for basic writing and related to all ages for written expression.

Note. The absence of comments for a particular CHC ability and achievement area (e.g., *Ga* and mathematics) indicates that the research reviewed either did not report any significant relations between the respective CHC ability and the achievement area, or that, if significant findings were reported, they were weak and were for only a limited number of studies. Comments in **bold** represent the CHC abilities that showed the strongest and most consistent relations with the respective achievement domain. Information in this table was reproduced from McGrew and Flanagan (1998), Flanagan, McGrew, and Ortiz (2000), and Flanagan et al. (2002) by Allyn & Bacon. Reprinted/adapted by permission.

narrow abilities within these broad CHC domains have been identified as related to writing achievement. Narrow abilities within the areas of *Gf, Gc, Gsm,* and *Gs* have demonstrated significant relationships with math achievement, and *Gf* (induction and general sequential reasoning) in particular has shown a stronger relationship to this academic area compared to its connections with the areas of reading and writing.

Identified weaknesses can be used to develop clinical hypotheses about the presence and nature of learning difficulties. However, it is important to note that limitations in cognitive/academic performance may be established by means other than standardized testing.

Intra-Achievement Discrepancy Procedure

A similar type of procedure is available when using the WJ III ACH; it is called the *intra-achievement discrepancy procedure.* This discrepancy procedure is described in detail in a companion volume, *Essentials of WJ III Tests of Achievement Assessment* (Mather, Wendling, & Woodcock, 2001).

The WJ III's intra-achievement discrepancy procedure can be used most effectively to identify an individual's relative academic strengths and weaknesses. You can use the information generated from this type of analysis to develop remedial strategies, educational plans, and specific academic interventions. In addition to the intra-achievement discrepancy procedure, the Age/Grade Profile may be particularly useful for this purpose.

DON'T FORGET

The WJ III's intra-achievement discrepancy procedure can be used most effectively to identify an individual's relative academic strengths and weaknesses.

Intra-Individual Discrepancy Procedure

When using both batteries together, another intra-ability discrepancy procedure is available; it is called the intra-individual discrepancy procedure. This procedure allows you to analyze an individual's cognitive and academic performance across the clusters of the WJ III COG and WJ III ACH and to explore co-varying cognitive and achievement strengths and weaknesses. A case study using the intra-individual discrepancy procedure is described in Chapter

7 of this book. This form of intra-
ability analysis can be used to examine an individual's performance
across the entire WJ III to determine if any relative strengths and
weaknesses exist.

> # CAUTION
>
> When an individual's cognitive and
> academic scores are combined in
> the intra-individual discrepancy pro-
> cedure, you should be aware that
> the magnitude of differences among
> test scores may be reduced from
> those observed in the separate in-
> tra-cognitive or intra-achievement
> discrepancy procedures

The intra-individual discrepancy
analysis is intended to help you
determine and document both
strengths and weaknesses in learning abilities, as well as to define how
these abilities are related to learning difficulties. For example, a reading problem may be caused by some underlying condition (such as poor phonological
awareness or poor memory) that may affect others areas as well (e.g., memorization of math facts). However, because the intra-individual discrepancy procedure is based on a larger mix of abilities (cognitive and achievement combined) it is possible that strengths or weaknesses that were found in the
intra-cognitive or intra-achievement discrepancy procedures may become at-
tenuated in the intra-individual discrepancy procedure. That is, when an individual's cognitive and academic scores are combined in one statistical mix, you
should be aware that the magnitude of differences between test scores will
change from what may have been observed in the separate intra-cognitive and
intra-achievement discrepancy procedures.

INTERPRETATION OF DISCREPANCIES

The WJ III includes several ability-achievement discrepancy procedures.
These are summarized in Rapid Reference 6.3. The General Intellectual Abil-
ity/Achievement discrepancy procedure is most conceptually similar to the
traditional IQ-achievement discrepancy model. The Predicted Achievement/
Achievement discrepancy model is the psychometrically preferred model
for predicting an individual's near-term academic performance. Because
many individuals with "specific" reading and writing impairments show a discrepancy between oral and written language abilities, the Oral Language Abil-
ity/Achievement discrepancy model can provide insight into possible oral lan-
guage-reading processing differences.

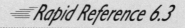

Rapid Reference 6.3

Types of Discrepancy Options Offered by the WJ III

Type of WJ III Discrepancy Analysis	Description
Intra-Ability Discrepancy Options	
Intra-achievement	This discrepancy analysis allows comparison of one area of academic achievement to the examinee's average performance in other achievement areas. An intra-achievement discrepancy is present within individuals who have specific achievement strengths or weaknesses. This type of information is an invaluable aid in instructional planning. Intra-achievement discrepancies can be calculated on four broad curricular areas or nine specific areas of academic performance.
Intracognitive	This discrepancy is present within individuals who have specific cognitive strengths or weaknesses. Equal interest exists in either a strength or a weakness in one ability relative to the average of all other cognitive abilities. This profile of discrepancies can document areas of strength and weakness, provide insights for program planning, and contribute to a deeper understanding of the types of tasks that will be especially easy or difficult for an individual compared to his or her other abilities.
Intra-individual	This discrepancy analysis reflects the amount of disparity among all cognitive and academic abilities. The bidirectional comparison examines the simultaneous relationship among various cognitive and academic skills. This procedure provides a more complete picture of an examinee's functioning, which, in turn, could lead to the selection of the most appropriate service delivery and intervention options.
Ability/Achievement Discrepancy Options	
GIA/ACH (Std) GIA/ACH (Ext)	The general intellectual ability/achievement discrepancies are based on the first principal component (g) of the tests included in the GIA–Standard Scale and the GIA–Extended Scale. Use of these scores provides a generalized index of intellectual ability as the predictor measure.

Oral Language/ Achievement	This discrepancy procedure compares oral language ability to academic performance and may be used to help substantiate the existence of a specific reading, math, or writing disability. Subjects with a significant negative discrepancy between oral language ability and achievement exhibit relative strengths in oral language with weaknesses in one or more areas of achievement.
Predicted Achievement/ Achievement	This discrepancy procedure can be used in each academic area to determine whether a subject is achieving commensurate with his or her current levels of associated cognitive abilities. This procedure uses differentially weighted composites to provide the best predictor of a given area of achievement at a given period of development.

Three intra-ability discrepancy procedures are available on the WJ III. Many professionals who use the WJ III prefer to use one or more of the intra-ability discrepancy procedures to help determine if an individual has LD. These procedures are particularly useful for describing patterns of strengths and weaknesses among an individual's abilities. These procedures are most appropriate when the purposes of the assessment are to determine why an individual has a difficulty. The intra-cognitive discrepancy procedure, described in Chapter 4, is particularly useful for determining if a problem in cognitive processing exists. When the WJ III COG is used in conjunction with the WJ III ACH, additional information can be gained by observing patterns of strengths and weaknesses in either the intra-individual discrepancy procedure, or by using the intra-achievement discrepancy procedure conjointly with the intra-cognitive discrepancy procedure. Either way, the discrepancy procedure(s) may be useful in helping explain how a cognitive difficulty relates to academic performance. When used appropriately, each of the WJ III discrepancy procedures provides a unique piece of information that can be used diagnostically to understand an individual. Rapid Reference 6.4 is a sample interpretation of the intra-cognitive, intra-achievement, and each of the three ability-achievement discrepancies for the same individual. This interpretation was derived from the Report Writer for the WJ III (Schrank & Woodcock, 2002). In this example, each of the discrepancies revealed some significant piece of information about the individual. Text printed in bold type is an interpretation of each discrepancy.

≡ Rapid Reference 6.4

Sample Interpretation of Significant Discrepancies for an Individual

SUMMARY

Naomi was referred for evaluation of a specific learning disability. Her overall intellectual ability is in the average range.

When compared to others at her age level, Naomi's performance is high average in processing speed; average in comprehension-knowledge, visual-spatial thinking, auditory processing, and phonemic awareness; low average in long-term retrieval, fluid reasoning, and short-term memory; and low in working memory. **When her cognitive abilities are compared, Naomi demonstrated a significant weakness in working memory.**

Naomi's oral language skills (oral expression and listening comprehension) are average when compared to the range of scores obtained by others at her age level. When compared to others at her age level, Naomi's academic skills and her ability to apply those skills are both within the low average range. Her knowledge and fluency with academic tasks are both within the average range.

Naomi's performance is low average in basic reading skills, reading comprehension, math reasoning, and written expression; and low in math calculation skills and basic writing skills. Her knowledge of phoneme-grapheme relationships is average. **When her achievement areas are compared, Naomi demonstrated a significant weakness in math calculation skills.**

To help determine if any ability-achievement discrepancies exist, comparisons were made among Naomi's cognitive, oral language, and achievement scores. When compared to her overall intellectual ability, Naomi's achievement is significantly lower than predicted in the area of math calculation skills. Based on a mix of the cognitive tasks associated with performance in the particular academic area and most relevant to the specific achievement domain, Naomi's achievement is also significantly lower than predicted in the area of math calculation skills. Also, Naomi's math calculation skills, basic writing skills, and written expression are significantly lower than would be predicted by her oral language ability.

SUMMARY

The year 1977 marked the operationalization of the ability-achievement discrepancy as a criterion for determination of a learning disability. That same year, the original Woodcock-Johnson Psycho-Educational Battery was published. Today, many professionals are moving away from the criterion of an ability-achievement discrepancy. For example, in "Rethinking Learning Disabilities," Lyon et al. suggest several alternatives to this model. Also, Flanagan, Ortiz, Alfonso, and Mascolo (2002) have proposed an operational definition of LD that allows for, but moves beyond, the concept of an ability-achievement discrepancy. The WJ III provides a tool to support current thinking about alternative models for determining the presence and severity of psychoeducational discrepancies.

Many professionals today are learning more about domain-specific processes and, therefore, are finding usefulness in the assessment of multiple abilities and how the abilities vary within an individual. That is, once an academic problem has been identified, the examiner attempts to determine the specific abilities or processing capacities that are affecting academic performance. The WJ III COG has many different measures that can help an evaluator determine the factors related to poor performance. As noted by Woodcock (1997); the WJ-R is based on a philosophy that the primary purpose of testing should be to find out more about the problem, not to determine an IQ (p. 235). The varied discrepancy procedures on the WJ III can help examiners accomplish this goal. In other words, the WJ III is based upon the belief that the diagnosis of learning disabilities should be multidimensional in nature, not based upon the findings from one single discrepancy procedure or one definitive score.

✍️ TEST YOURSELF 🐟

1. The development and subsequent revisions of the Woodcock-Johnson parallels the enactment and implementation of the Education of All Handicapped Children Act. True or False?

2. In what year did the US Office of Education adopt the criterion of an *ability-achievement discrepancy* as a criterion for identification of a specific learning disability?

   (a) 1973

   (b) 1975

   (c) 1977

   (d) 1979

3. There are several alternative procedures for determining the presence and severity of psychoeducational discrepancies in the WJ III. True or False?

4. There are two fundamentally different types of discrepancy procedures on the WJ III---intra-ability and ability-achievement. True or False?

5. Which of the following is NOT an ability-achievement discrepancy procedure?

   (a) Predicted Achievement/Achievement

   (b) General Intellectual Ability/Achievement

   (c) Oral Language Ability/Achievement

   (d) Intra-Individual

6. All WJ III discrepancy procedures are based on actual norms. True or False?

7. Which of the following discrepancy procedures is best suited to predict an individual's academic performance based upon his or her levels of associated cognitive abilities?

   (a) Predicted Achievement/Achievement

   (b) General Intellectual Ability/Achievement

   (c) Oral Language Ability/Achievement

   (d) Intra-Individual

8. Which of the following discrepancy procedures most closely matches the traditional IQ-achievement discrepancy model?

   (a) Predicted Achievement/Achievement

   (b) General Intellectual Ability/Achievement

   (c) Oral Language Ability/Achievement

   (d) Intra-Individual

9. **The Oral Language Ability/Achievement discrepancy procedure has particular relevance for helping distinguish between individuals with adequate oral language capabilities, but poor reading and writing abilities.** True or False?

10. **When interpreted diagnostically, each of the WJ III discrepancies can provide information about an individual.** True or False?

Answers: 1.True; 2. c; 3.True; 4.True; 5. d; 6.True; 7. a; 8. b; 9.True; 10.True

Seven

ILLUSTRATIVE CASE REPORTS

This chapter includes two illustrative case studies of individuals who were referred for comprehensive psychoeducational evaluations.

The first case study involves a cognitive assessment of a fourth-grader aged 9 years 7 months. The information presented for this case includes data from the WJ III COG only. Additionally, because the assessment focuses on cognitive functioning, only intracognitive discrepancies are presented and discussed. The format and interpretation of this report is organized around Cattell-Horn-Carroll (CHC) theory.

The second case study involves a comprehensive psychoeducational assessment of a sixth-grader, aged 11 years, suspected of having a learning disability. The information presented for this case includes data from both the WJ III COG and the WJ III ACH, as well as reports provided by the student's parent and teacher. One section of this case study focuses on her cognitive performance and organizes data (e.g., standard scores, percentile ranks, and qualitative descriptors of performance) according to Woodcock's Cognitive Performance Model (CPM; see Mather & Woodcock, 2001). Information on the conditions that facilitate or inhibit her cognitive or academic performance can be gleaned from the parent's report, the teacher's report, and the "Test Session Observation Checklist" on the WJ III Test Records. Following the discussion of cognitive performance, all relevant achievement data are presented. Whereas the cognitive section of this report presents score information and interprets strengths and weaknesses within the context of CHC domains, the achievement section of the report presents a more focused interpretation of performance within the context of Woodcock's Information Processing Model (IPM; see Mather & Woodcock, 2001). The interpretation of data from this perspective illustrates how the identified strengths and weaknesses interact to affect real-world performance.

The case studies presented here are based on the administration of both the Standard and Extended Batteries of the WJ III COG, and, in the case of the second report, the entire WJ III ACH as well. The complete set of WJ III tests are used for the case studies because the reports are intended to be teaching tools. The case studies are intended to help you become familiar with interpretation of the various tests, clusters, and composites that comprise the WJ III. In clinical practice, however, you should organize your assessments to respond to specific referral concerns and should not consider the administration of the entire WJ III a recommended standard. Also, unlike with the following case studies, your interpretation should typically focus on the cluster level, unless significant differences between tests that comprise a cluster warrant special emphasis on the narrow abilities measured by the component tests (see Chapter 4).

It is also important to note how performance on the WJ III tests and clusters is described. Throughout the case reports, readers will note numerous examples of qualitative analysis of performance. Cluster performance is described primarily in terms of peer comparison scores (standard scores [SSs] and corresponding percentile ranks [PRs]), because cluster standard scores are used in the intra-cognitive and ability/achievement discrepancy procedures. For the academic areas, developmental-level information is included. Analysis of performance at the narrow ability or individual test level is demonstrated primarily through criterion-referenced interpretation. Rapid Reference 4.6 provides a list of labels that can be used to transform the WJ III RPI scores into the criterion-referenced terminology used in these reports.

CAUTION

The case studies presented in this chapter are for illustrative purposes only. To help you understand the nature of the broad and narrow abilities measured by the WJ III, each case study describes the individual's performance at the test level as well as the cluster level. Typically, however, you should follow the principle of cluster interpretation. That is, you should focus interpretation at the cluster level only, unless significant differences among the tests that comprise a cluster warrant a distinction between the individual's performance on the narrow abilities measured by each test.

CASE REPORT #1

Name: Mason J.   School: Jefferson Elementary
Date of Birth: 3/25/91   Teacher: Mrs. Meyers
Age: 9-7   Grade: 4.2
Sex: Male   Examiner: Robert Johnson
Date of Testing: 10/27/2000

Reason for Referral

Mason J. was referred by his mother for a comprehensive evaluation. She reported that although Mason is passing all of his classes, he requires an excessive amount of time to study and complete his homework. She reported that this additional time is not due to inattentiveness, perfectionism, or any other behavioral attribute. She requested a comprehensive evaluation to determine whether his difficulties are due to an underlying cognitive weakness.

Background Information

Mason currently resides with his biological mother and father and two younger siblings, aged 4 and 6. Maternal report indicated that Mason was the product of a normal, full-term pregnancy. Although Mason's motor skills (e.g., sitting upright, crawling, and walking) developed later than for most children, he achieved other developmental milestones (e.g., language) within normal limits.

Tests Administered

Woodcock-Johnson III Tests of Cognitive Abilities, Standard and Extended Batteries

Assessment of Cognitive Functioning

Mason's general intellectual ability is in the average range, as shown by his GIA-Ext standard score of 90 (88-92) and corresponding percentile rank (26). His performance across various domains of cognitive ability is described in the following sections and summarized in Table 7.1.

Table 7.1 Woodcock-Johnson III Tests of Cognitive Abilities, Compuscore Version 1.1b Score Report for Mason J.

CLUSTER/Test	RAW	AE	EASY	to	DIFF	RPI	PR	SS (68% BAND)
GIA (Ext)	-	8-6	7-2		10-3	81/90	26	90 (88-92)
VERBAL ABILITY (Ext)	-	8-1	6-10		9-7	75/90	24	89 (86-93)
THINKING ABILITY (Ext)	-	8-5	6-7		12-4	85/90	30	92 (89-95)
COG EFFICIENCY (Ext)	-	9-2	8-2		10-5	86/90	41	97 (93-100)
COMP-KNOWLEDGE (Gc)	-	8-1	6-10		9-7	75/90	24	89 (86-93)
L-T RETRIEVAL (Glr)	-	7-5	5-3		13-0	83/90	13	83 (79-87)
VIS-SPATIAL THINK (Gv)	-	10-0	6-10		>25	91/90	55	102 (97-106)
AUDITORY PROCESS (Ga)	-	8-11	6-7		13-6	88/90	41	97 (91-102)
FLUID REASONING (Gf)	-	8-1	7-1		9-9	76/90	27	91 (87-94)
PROCESS SPEED (Gs)	-	10-7	9-7		11-9	96/90	76	111 (107-115)
SHORT-TERM MEM (Gsm)	-	7-3	6-5		8-5	58/90	19	87 (82-91)
PHONEMIC AWARE	-	8-6	6-2		12-10	86/90	35	94 (88-100)
WORKING MEMORY	-	6-8	6-0		7-8	40/90	8	79 (75-83)
BROAD ATTENTION	-	8-1	6-10		9-9	76/90	19	87 (83-91)
COGNITIVE FLUENCY	-	8-1	6-10		9-8	76/90	22	88 (86-91)
EXEC PROCESSES	-	9-4	7-7		12-2	89/90	46	98 (95-101)
Verbal Comprehension	-	8-3	7-0		9-9	77/90	27	91 (85-96)
Visual-Auditory Learning	29-E	6-10	5-5		9-3	73/90	11	81 (78-85)
Spatial Relations	66-D	11-3	7-3		>25	93/90	62	105 (100-110)
Sound Blending	16	8-0	6-2		10-9	82/90	32	93 (87-99)
Concept Formation	16-D	7-9	6-10		9-0	68/90	24	89 (85-93)
Visual Matching	38-2	10-0	9-3		10-9	94/90	62	105 (100-109)
Numbers Reversed	8	6-11	6-4		7-10	46/90	17	86 (81-91)
Incomplete Words	20	9-5	6-1		21	90/90	49	100 (93-106)

(continued)

Table 7.1 (Continued)

CLUSTER/Test	RAW	AE	EASY to DIFF		RPI	PR	SS (68% BAND)
Auditory Work Memory	7	6-3	5-3	7-5	34/90	6	76 (71-82)
General Information	-	7-11	6-9	9-5	73/90	22	88 (83-94)
Retrieval Fluency	53	9-5	4-11	>30	90/90	48	99 (93-105)
Picture Recognition	45-D	9-2	6-5	16-2	89/90	47	99 (94-103)
Auditory Attention	37	10-8	7-1	>20	92/90	60	104 (97-111)
Analysis-Synthesis	20-D	8-6	7-4	10-10	83/90	37	95 (91-100)
Decision Speed	31	11-9	10-3	13-9	98/90	85	116 (110-121)
Memory for Words	15	7-8	6-6	9-1	69/90	28	91 (85-98)
Rapid Picture Naming	69	5-9	5-2	6-5	7/90	6	76 (75-78)
Planning	-	13-0	4-9	>28	91/90	73	109 (93-125)
Pair Cancellation	60	10-9	9-4	12-7	96/90	71	108 (106-111)

DISCREPANCIES	STANDARD SCORES			DISCREPANCY		Significant at
	Actual	Predicted	Difference	PR	SD	+ or −1.50 SD (SEE)
Intra-Cognitive						
COMP-KNOWLEDGE (Gc)	89	96	−7	32	−0.48	No
L-T RETRIEVAL (Glr)	83	96	−13	16	−1.01	No
VIS-SPATIAL THINK (Gv)	102	96	+6	67	+0.43	No
AUDITORY PROCESS (Ga)	97	95	+2	53	+0.08	No
FLUID REASONING (Gf)	91	95	−4	35	−0.37	No
PROCESS SPEED (Gs)	111	94	+17	88	+1.19	No
SHORT-TERM MEM (Gsm)	87	96	−9	22	−0.77	No
PHONEMIC AWARE	94	96	−2	46	−0.10	No
WORKING MEMORY	79	96	−17	8	−1.40	No

Note. Norms based on age 9-7.

Assessment of Comprehension-Knowledge (Gc)

Comprehension-Knowledge (*Gc*) refers to an individual's breadth and depth of knowledge, including verbal communication, information, and reasoning with previously learned procedures. Mason's *Gc* ability was assessed through tasks that required him to identify pic-

> **DON'T FORGET**
> ....
> Use the Standard Score/Percentile Rank Profile to compare performance on tests that comprise each of the CHC clusters. When the tests that comprise a cluster differ statistically, it may be more appropriate to describe the individual's performance at the test level.

tures of familiar and unfamiliar objects; listen to words presented by the examiner and provide an appropriate synonym or antonym; and complete a four-part analogy based on the three parts already given. Taken together, these tasks provide a measure of Mason's knowledge of vocabulary as well as his ability to reason using lexical (word) knowledge. Additionally, Mason was required to respond to a series of questions in which he had to identify where he would find a specific object and, later, what he would do with a series of specific objects. Overall, Mason obtained a Comprehension-Knowledge score of 89 (86-93), which is ranked at the 24th percentile and classified as Low Average, suggesting that his language development, general fund of information, and ability to reason using lexical knowledge is within normal limits, but below that of 76% of his same-age peers.

Assessment of Long-Term Retrieval (Glr)

Long-Term Retrieval (*Glr*) is a broad ability that involves an individual's ability to store information efficiently and retrieve it later through association. Mason's *Glr* ability was assessed through tasks that required him to learn and recall rebuses (i.e., pictographic representations of words) and to name as many examples possible from a series of three categories (e.g., things to eat or drink, first names of people, and animals) within a 1-min time period. More specifically, these tasks assessed Mason's ability to learn, store, and retrieve a series of associations (Associative Memory) as well as his ability to fluently retrieve information from stored knowledge (Ideational Fluency). Mason's Long-Term Retrieval cluster score of 83 (79-87) is ranked at the 13th percentile and classified as Low Average. However, Mason's performance on the associative memory task (Visual-Auditory Learning) suggests that his efficiency in transferring and storing information to be recalled later is limited. Moreover, although Mason's efficiency in retrieving information (i.e., Retrieval Fluency) was estimated to be Average, his performance appears to have been facilitated by testing conditions. For example, Mason's highest level of performance was demonstrated when he was required to provide names of animals quickly; however, the testing room in which this task was administered had pictures of animals hanging on the wall, which may have facilitated his performance. Consequently, although Mason's ability to fluently retrieve information was estimated to be within normal limits, this may be an overestimate especially in light of his performance on other retrieval measures requiring fluent responding. More specifically, Mason demonstrated low performance on a task requiring him to fluently retrieve names of pictured objects. A review of Mason's responses on this test revealed that although he was able to accurately name all presented objects with one exception (i.e., he labeled a cup a "glass"), his naming speed was very limited. Mason's overall performance in the domain of long-term retrieval is notable because some individuals with similar retrieval impairments demonstrate difficulties in relating prior knowledge to new knowledge, which can impact performance in a variety of academic areas (e.g., reading, writing, and mathematics).

Assessment of Visual-Spatial Thinking (Gv)

Visual-Spatial Thinking (Gv) includes spatial orientation, the ability to analyze and synthesize visual stimuli, and the ability to hold and manipulate mental images. Mason's Gv ability was assessed through tasks that required him to identify two or three pieces that form a complete target shape and recognize a subset of previously presented pictures within a field of distracting pictures. These tasks primarily assessed Mason's ability to perceive and manipulate visual patterns as well as his visual memory of objects or pictures. Mason obtained an overall Gv cluster score of 102 (97-106), which is ranked at the 55th percentile and classified as Average. Mason's variation in performance on Gv tasks was not statistically significant, indicating uniform ability within this domain. Given Mason's low average performance in the area of long-term retrieval, he may benefit from drawing upon his visual processing abilities when attempting to encode information. Specifically, Mason may find that pairing information to be learned with *meaningful* visual stimuli may facilitate the efficiency with which he initially stores information, which, in turn, could facilitate later retrieval.

Assessment of Auditory Processing (Ga)

Auditory Processing (*Ga*) involves the ability to discriminate, analyze, and synthesize auditory stimuli. Mason's auditory processing was assessed through one task that required him to listen to a series of syllables or phonemes and then blend the sounds into a word, and another task that required him to listen to individual words amid increasing auditory distortion. Mason obtained a *Ga* cluster score of 97 (91-102), which is ranked at the 41st percentile and classified as Average. Mason's performance within this domain is consistent with his performance on another phonetic coding task involving analysis of sounds. This additional task required Mason to identify a complete word that was initially presented with one or more phonemes missing. Overall, Mason's ability to process, analyze, and synthesize auditory information suggests a *potential* for success on several academic tasks such as reading decoding and spelling.

Assessment of Fluid Reasoning (Gf)

Fluid Reasoning (*Gf*) involves the ability to reason and solve problems that often involve unfamiliar information or procedures. *Gf* is generally manifested in an individual's ability to reorganize, transform, and use information to solve novel problems. These abilities may include figuring out how to organize math problems by using information provided within the problem, or using specific information in a reading passage to reach general conclusions are examples of reasoning ability. Mason's *Gf* ability was assessed through tasks that required him to derive rules for a set of presented stimulus items and analyze the parts of an incomplete logic puzzle and identify the missing parts. More specifically, these tasks assessed Mason's ability to utilize categorical reasoning based on principles of inductive logic and his ability to reason and draw conclusions from given conditions. Mason obtained a *Gf* cluster score of 91 (87-94), which is ranked at the 27th percentile and classified as Average. In addition to these tasks, Mason was required to trace a pattern while neither lifting his pencil nor retracing any lines. This task primarily assessed Mason's ability to determine, select, and apply solutions using forethought. Mason's performance on this task, and more specifically within the Fluid Reasoning domain, suggests that his ability to solve novel problems using reasoning and exercising forethought is Average and at a level expected of most individuals his age.

Assessment of Processing Speed (Gs)

Processing Speed (Gs) involves the speed and efficiency in performing automatic or very simple cognitive tasks. Mason's Gs ability was assessed through tasks that required him to quickly locate and circle two identical numbers in a row of six numbers and quickly locate the two pictures in a row of pictures that are most conceptually similar. These tasks primarily measured the speed at which Mason could make visual/symbol discriminations and his ability to process simple concepts and rapidly make correct conceptual decisions, respectively. In addition to these tasks, Mason was required to locate and mark a repeated pattern as quickly as possible. Mason's overall Gs cluster score of 111 (107-115, 76th percentile; High Average) suggests that he not only can perform simple cognitive tasks automatically, but can also sustain attention and exercise interference control when faced with distracting stimuli.

Assessment of Short-Term Memory (Gsm)

Short-Term Memory (Gsm) is the ability to hold information in immediate awareness and use it within a few seconds. Mason's Gsm ability was assessed through one task that required him to hold a span of numbers in immediate awareness while performing a mental operation on it, and another task that required him to repeat lists of unrelated words in the correct sequence. These tasks primarily measured auditory memory span and working memory respectively. Mason obtained a Gsm cluster score of 87 (82–91), which is ranked at the 19th percentile and classified as Low Average. Mason's performance suggests that although his ability to hold information in immediate awareness is average, his performance is limited when he is required to perform some operation on the retained information. As demands on working memory increase, Mason may have difficulty performing the task. This hypothesis is supported by Mason's limited performance on an additional Gsm measure wherein he was required to listen to a series that contained alternating digits and words, and then to repeat the information, presenting the objects in sequential order followed by the digits in sequential order. Overall, Mason's weaknesses in the domain of short-term memory will very likely impact his performance in reading, spelling, writing, and the retention of oral directions. Specifically, Mason may have difficulty when academic work in these areas requires use of working memory capacity.

Assessment of Executive Functions

The WJ III clinical clusters provide information regarding an individual's allocation of attentional resources, working memory, planning, problem solving, response inhibition, self-monitoring and regulation, and his or her ability to maintain mental flexibility when solving problems. Mason's ability to strategically plan, inhibit responses, and maintain flexibility when solving problems (Executive Processes; SS = 98 [95-101]) is average. Comparatively, Mason's attentional abilities (Broad Attention; SS = 87 [83-91]) and the ease and speed with which he performs cognitive tasks (Cognitive Fluency; SS = 88 [86-91]) are low average. An analysis of Mason's performance within the Broad Attention Cluster suggests that although Mason's selective attention, sustained attention, and attentional capacity are within normal limits, his ability to divide his attention is limited. Mason's difficulty with divided attention is a working memory limitation (Working Memory; SS = 79 [75-83]; Low), because working memory involves an individual's ability to temporarily store and perform a set of operations on information that requires divided attention.

Summary

Mason is a male aged 9-7 who was referred for a comprehensive assessment of cognitive functioning by his mother, who was concerned with the high level of effort and large amount of time he was spending studying and completing schoolwork. Mason's general intellectual ability is in the Average range. In terms of specific cognitive processes, Mason's performance is average in visual-spatial thinking, auditory processing, fluid reasoning, and processing speed, and low average in comprehension-knowledge, long-term retrieval, and short-term memory. Despite specific, circumscribed, and observed performance problems, no significant discrepancies were found among Mason's cognitive abilities.

Although Mason's executive processes and cognitive fluency are generally within normal limits, his working memory capacity and attentional resources are limited to average. Limitations in these areas may impact functioning in the acquisition and application of higher-level reading, writing, and mathematics skills. Additionally, such limitations may partly explain why Mason is spending an excessive amount of time studying and completing his homework. Specifically, Mason may be attempting to compensate for his memory and attentional limitations by completing his work in small, manageable steps, or by applying effective but time-consuming strategies (e.g., writing down every step in a math problem). Although such strategies may circumvent his memory limitations, it would be beneficial to provide Mason with additional, specific strategies to encode, transform, and retrieve information. Mason's ability in the area of visual-spatial thinking should be utilized in this regard (e.g., pairing information to be learned with meaningful visual stimuli). Additionally, Mason's reasoning abilities should be integrated into the generation of new strategies that can be used to facilitate and consolidate new learning. This will not only provide Mason with a broader range of strategies to use when approaching new tasks, but may also reduce the amount of time he currently spends studying and completing classroom assignments. In addition to these recommendations, a comprehensive assessment of Mason's academic achievement should be undertaken, with a specific focus on his academic fluency, to determine the extent to which his cognitive abilities may be impacting his academic performance.

CASE REPORT #2

Name: Kayla W.   School: Jefferson Elementary
Date of Birth: 11/10/89   Teacher: Mr. Smith
Age: 11-0   Grade: 6.2
Sex: Female   Examiner: Bob Johnson
Date of Testing: 11/07/2000

Reason for Referral

Kayla was referred for a psychoeducational evaluation by her teacher, Mr. Smith, because of concerns about her academic performance, particularly in the areas of mathematics and writing. Mr. Smith reported that Kayla requires a significant amount of one-on-one attention when completing classroom tasks. According to Mr. Smith, Kayla's academic performance in the classroom when she does not receive frequent assistance is markedly impaired relative to that of her classmates. That is, although Kayla will make an initial attempt when presented with difficult tasks, she gives up rather easily and requires prompting and guidance to follow through on her initial efforts. Because Kayla's instructional program has been consistently modified from first through sixth grade, and she has not appeared to have obtained commensurate academic gains, Mr. Smith requested formal testing to identify the underlying causes of her learning difficulties.

≡ Rapid Reference 7.1

Include information on the conditions or individual characteristics that can facilitate or inhibit cognitive and academic performance. For children, some of this information can be gathered from parents. (The Individuals with Disabilities Education Act [IDEA] requires inclusion of information from the child's parents in an assessment for a placement decision.) The following is a list of parent questions, organized by categories, that have been found useful in eliciting facilitator/inhibitor information.

Current Home and Health Status

- With whom does your child live?
- How many other children live in the same home?
- What is the highest grade-level completed by each parent with whom your child lives?
- Are any languages other than English spoken in your home?
- Have there been any recent changes in family life (i.e., birth of a child, divorce of parents, move to a new home)?
- What is your child's overall physical health?
- Has your child ever sustained a head injury?
- Has your child ever had a serious illness?
- Does your child have seizures?
- How would you describe your child's vision?
- Has your child had a recent vision test?
- How would you describe your child's hearing?
- Has your child had a recent hearing test?
- How much sleep does your child typically get each night?
- How soundly does your child sleep?
- Has your child shown any recent changes in appetite?
- Does your child frequently complain about not feeling well?
- Has any other member of your child's immediate family experienced personal, social, or learning problems?

Birth History

- What was the birth mother's condition during pregnancy?
- How would you describe your child's birth?
- What was your child's condition immediately after birth?

(continued)

Infancy and Early Childhood

- How would you describe your child's temperament (personality) during infancy and early childhood?
- How would you rate the development of your child's early motor skills, such as sitting up, crawling, and learning to walk?
- How would you rate your child's early language development, such as first words, asking simple questions, and talking in sentences?
- Did your child have frequent ear infections (more than four in a 12-month period)?

Child's Preschool History

- Did your child attend preschool?
- During ages 3–5, how would you describe your child's cognitive development, such as counting, knowledge of the alphabet, and general knowledge and understanding?
- During ages 3–5, how would you describe your child's social development, such as ability to play with others, development of friendships, and relationship with adults?
- How difficult to manage was his or her behavior during the preschool years?

School History

- Has your child ever repeated a grade?
- Has your child ever received special educational services, such as resource-room instruction, speech therapy, or an individualized education program (IEP)?
- Do you believe your child has learning problems?
- If you believe your child has learning problems, how long have you been concerned about this?

Current Temperament and Mood

- How would you describe your child's temperament (personality)?
- How would you describe your child's typical mood?
- How consistent is his or her mood?

Current Behaviors

- What is your child's attitude toward school?
- How would you describe your child's level of effort toward schoolwork?
- When helping or working at home, how attentive is your child to details?
- How would you describe your child's attention span?
- How would you describe your child's listening ability?

- How would you describe your child's follow-through on homework?
- How would you describe your child's level of organization?
- How would you describe your child's response to tasks that are difficult for him or her?
- How well does your child maintain personal belongings?
- How does your child typically respond to distractions?
- How would you describe your child's remembering/forgetfulness?
- What is your child's typical activity level when watching television, eating meals, or doing homework?
- What is your child's typical activity level in social situations outside the home?
- Can your child play or work quietly when required?
- What is your child's typical style of motor activity?
- How much talking does your child do?
- How well does your child interact with peers?
- How good is your child at taking turns?
- Are there any behavior problems at home? If so, what, specifically?

Parent's Report

Kayla lives with her mother, Jackie W. Two other children, aged 17 and 14, live in the same home.

According to her mother, Kayla is usually in good health and is physically fit. Ms. W. reported that Kayla's vision is normal, and her vision was tested recently (03/2000). Ms. W. reported that Kayla's hearing is normal, but Kayla has not had a recent hearing test.

During pregnancy, Kayla's mother had no significant health problems. Kayla's delivery was normal. Immediately after birth, Kayla was healthy.

Kayla's mother remembers Kayla as a determined but shy and fearful infant and toddler. Her early motor skills, such as sitting up, crawling, and learning to walk, developed normally. Her early language development, such as first words, asking simple questions, and talking in sentences, seemed to be typical.

Kayla did not attend preschool. She seemed to learn things more slowly or with more difficulty than other children did. She seemed to have more difficulty developing social skills than most other children. No atypical behavior management problems were recalled.

Kayla received special educational services beginning at age 6. She is currently in a modified sixth-grade program. Ms. W. believes that Kayla has learning problems (especially with math, spelling, and reading). She has been concerned about these problems for about 5 years.

At the time of this assessment, Ms. W. described Kayla as independent, happy, and caring. She said that Kayla generally likes school, although it seems she does not really try to succeed. Kayla has many positive qualities. She always, or almost always, remembers what she is supposed to do and keeps her personal belongings in order. She usually maintains attention during tasks and play activities, listens when spoken to directly, and organizes her tasks and activities.

Kayla usually reacts normally to distractions and adapts to them. Her activity level and style of motor activity are similar to those of other girls her age. Kayla can play or work quietly when asked to do so. Her social interaction skills are typical of girls her age.

Kayla's mother reported that at home, Kayla often fails to give close attention to details or makes careless mistakes. She frequently does not follow through on instructions and fails to finish her homework. She often avoids, dislikes, or is reluctant to engage in tasks that are difficult for her. (See Rapid Reference 7.1.)

Teacher's Report

Mr. Smith, Kayla's teacher, described Kayla as reserved but insecure and introverted. He said that she needs more one-to-one attention but completes about as much schoolwork as other girls her age.

Mr. Smith reported that Kayla demonstrates a number of behaviors that serve to facilitate her academic performance. For example, Kayla always, or almost always, listens when spoken to directly and organizes her tasks and activities. She usually keeps her assignments and school supplies in order and remembers what she is supposed to do. Kayla reacts normally to distractions and adapts to them.

Although Kayla usually remains seated when expected to, she often seems lethargic. She usually attempts but gives up easily when confronted with difficult tasks. She often has difficulty maintaining attention to tasks and fails to give close attention to details or makes mistakes in her schoolwork.

≣ Rapid Reference 7.2

For school-aged individuals, information on the conditions or individual characteristics that can facilitate or inhibit cognitive and academic performance can also be gathered from the individual's teacher. (The Individuals with Disabilities Education Act [IDEA] requires inclusion of information from the child's teacher in an assessment for a placement decision.) The following is a suggested list of teacher questions, organized by categories, that is useful in eliciting facilitator and inhibitor information.

- How would you describe the individual's level of academic achievement in each area of instruction?
- What grade level of instruction is being provided in each academic area?
- How would you describe this student's temperament (personality) and mood? How consistent is this student's mood?
- How much one-to-one attention does this student require in the classroom?
- How much schoolwork does this student typically complete?
- How attentive is this student to details?
- How would you describe this student's ability to sustain attention?
- How would you describe this student's listening ability?
- How would you describe this student's follow-through on schoolwork?
- How would you describe this student's level of organization?
- How would you describe this student's response to tasks that are difficult for him or her?
- How well does this student maintain personal belongings?
- How does this student typically respond to distractions?
- How would you describe this student's remembering/forgetfulness?
- What is this student's typical activity level when seated?
- Does this student usually remain seated when expected to?
- Can this student play or work quietly when required?
- What is this student's typical style of motor activity?
- How much talking does this student do?
- How does this student typically respond to questions asked orally?
- How well does this student interact with peers?
- How good is this student at taking turns?
- Does the individual demonstrate any behavior problems in the classroom? If so, what specifically? How serious are the behaviors? How disruptive to others are the behaviors?

DON'T FORGET

For school-aged individuals, don't forget to include an observation of the student's performance in the classroom. (The Individuals with Disabilities Education Act [IDEA] requires that a person other than the child's primary teacher observe the student's performance in the classroom in an assessment for a placement decision.)

These descriptions are based on Mr. Smith's typical observations of Kayla over the past month. Mr. Smith is most concerned about the amount of one-to-one attention Kayla requires in the classroom.

Kayla is being instructed in reading at the fifth-grade level. She is being instructed at the fourth-grade level in math and writing. (See Rapid Reference 7.2.)

Classroom Observation

Kayla was observed in the classroom on November 1, 2000, doing individual math seatwork. When compared to another female student who was identified as typical, Kayla was observed as having more off-task behaviors. During the 15-min observation, the comparison student was off task three times; Kayla was off task five times. Inattentive behaviors (looking around the classroom) and withdrawn behaviors (daydreaming, playing with pen) were observed, but these behaviors were not serious or disruptive to others. The primary problem behavior observed was withdrawal. According to Kayla's teacher, her behavior during this observation was typical of her.

Tests Administered

Woodcock-Johnson III Tests of Cognitive Abilities, Extended Battery
Woodcock-Johnson III Tests of Achievement, Form B, Extended Battery

Test Session Observations

Kayla's conversational proficiency throughout the testing session appeared typical for her age level. Behaviorally, Kayla was cooperative and her activity level was commensurate with that of same-age peers. Rapport was readily established and maintained throughout the testing sessions. Specifically, Kayla appeared at ease, comfortable, and attentive to tasks during the examinations.

Kayla responded promptly and with care to test questions. However, she tended to give up rather easily when presented with difficult tasks. The current assessment appears to represent a valid estimate of Kayla's cognitive and academic functioning.

Assessment of Cognitive Functioning

Kayla's general intellectual ability (GIA-Ext score of 91 [89-93]) is ranked at the 27th percentile and is classified as Average. An examination of Kayla's performance within and across several cognitive domains appears in the following sections. Her scores are reported in Table 7.2.

Verbal Ability

Kayla's performance in the domain of Comprehension-Knowledge (Gc) primarily reflects the breadth and depth of her acquired (verbal) knowledge as well as her ability to reason with that knowledge using previously learned procedures. Kayla's Gc ability was assessed through expressive vocabulary tasks wherein she was required to verbally identify pictures of familiar and unfamiliar objects and provide synonyms or antonyms for a series of words. To assess the degree to which she could reason with verbally based information, Kayla was required to provide a word that completed a four-part analogy. Kayla's performance on these tasks indicates that her knowledge of vocabulary and her ability to reason using word knowledge is within normal limits. Similarly, Kayla demonstrated average performance when required to answer questions relating to where she would find specific objects (e.g., a roof) and what she would do with specific objects (e.g., a dictionary). This performance suggests that her general fund of information is commensurate with that of same-age peers. Kayla's verbal abilities and fund of prior knowledge (Comprehension-Knowledge; SS = 93 [89-96]; Average) suggest that she has learned to apply new information in a variety of environments, particularly academic ones.

Thinking Abilities

The thinking abilities act upon information placed in short-term memory that cannot be processed automatically. Thinking and new learning occur through the effective use and application of Long-Term Retrieval (Glr), Visual-Spatial Thinking (Gv), Auditory Processing (Ga), and Fluid Reasoning (Gf).

Long-Term Retrieval (Glr). Kayla's performance in the domain of Long-

Table 7.2 Woodcock-Johnson III Tests of Cognitive Abilities and Tests of Achievement, Compuscore Version 1.1b Score Report for Kayla W.

CLUSTER/Test	RAW	GE	EASY to DIFF		RPI	PR	SS (68% BAND)	AE
GIA (Ext)	-	4.4	2.4	7.2	81/90	27	91 (89-93)	9-9
VERBAL ABILITY (Ext)	-	4.8	3.3	6.6	79/90	31	93 (89-96)	10-2
THINKING ABILITY (Ext)	-	3.6	1.5	8.4	82/90	25	90 (87-92)	9-1
COG EFFICIENCY (Ext)	-	5.4	4.0	7.1	84/90	36	95 (90-99)	10-9
COMP-KNOWLEDGE (Gc)	-	4.8	3.3	6.6	79/90	31	93 (89-96)	10-2
L-T RETRIEVAL (Glr)	-	3.0	K.9	13.7	84/90	17	86 (81-90)	8-9
VIS-SPATIAL THINK (Gv)	-	4.8	1.6	13.0	87/90	39	96 (92-100)	10-0
AUDITORY PROCESS (Ga)	-	4.2	1.2	10.6	86/90	36	95 (90-100)	9-9
FLUID REASONING (Gf)	-	3.2	2.0	5.0	65/90	20	87 (84-90)	8-6
PROCESS SPEED (Gs)	-	7.2	5.8	9.1	95/90	66	106 (102-110)	12-5
SHORT-TERM MEM (Gsm)	-	3.1	2.0	4.7	59/90	17	86 (80-92)	8-3
PHONEMIC AWARE	-	9.3	3.6	14.3	94/90	71	108 (102-114)	14-5
PHONEMIC AWARE III	-	5.8	2.5	12.5	89/90	47	99 (95-103)	11-5
WORKING MEMORY	-	1.7	K.9	2.6	21/90	2	71 (66-75)	6-10
BROAD ATTENTION	-	2.2	1.2	3.6	45/90	2	70 (66-74)	7-7
COGNITIVE FLUENCY	-	5.2	3.4	7.4	84/90	35	94 (91-97)	10-4
EXEC PROCESSES	-	3.6	2.1	6.0	74/90	16	85 (83-88)	9-0
KNOWLEDGE	-	5.4	3.9	7.2	84/90	38	96 (92-99)	10-7
ORAL LANGUAGE (Ext)	-	5.9	3.4	10.1	89/90	47	99 (96-102)	11-4
ORAL EXPRESSION	-	6.2	3.3	10.6	90/90	50	100 (95-105)	11-9
LISTENING COMP	-	5.6	3.5	9.7	88/90	44	98 (94-101)	11-0
TOTAL ACHIEVEMENT	-	3.4	2.7	4.4	41/90	9	80 (79-82)	8-9
BROAD READING	-	4.0	3.3	4.9	47/90	18	86 (84-88)	9-4
BROAD MATH	-	3.3	2.4	4.3	39/90	5	76 (73-79)	8-9
BROAD WRITTEN LANG	-	2.9	2.1	3.9	38/90	4	74 (71-78)	8-2

BASIC READING SKILLS	-	3.3	2.7	4.0	29/90	15	85 (83-86)	8-7
READING COMP	-	3.5	2.6	5.1	63/90	16	85 (82-88)	8-11
MATH CALC SKILLS	-	2.7	1.9	3.7	33/90	1	66 (62-70)	8-1
MATH REASONING	-	3.4	2.7	4.2	30/90	9	80 (76-83)	8-10
BASIC WRITING SKILLS	-	2.7	2.1	3.4	19/90	4	74 (71-77)	8-0
WRITTEN EXPRESSION	-	3.1	2.1	4.6	55/90	7	78 (74-82)	8-7
ACADEMIC SKILLS	-	3.0	2.5	3.6	15/90	3	71 (69-74)	8-3
ACADEMIC FLUENCY	-	4.3	3.3	5.5	63/90	20	87 (85-89)	9-9
ACADEMIC APPS	-	3.3	2.5	4.6	55/90	13	83 (80-86)	8-10
ACADEMIC KNOWLEDGE	-	5.1	3.6	6.7	81/90	34	94 (89-98)	10-2
PHON/GRAPH KNOW	-	3.0	2.1	4.9	63/90	21	88 (86-90)	8-6
Verbal Comprehension	-	3.9	2.6	5.5	67/90	20	87 (83-92)	9-4
Visual-Auditory Learning	19-E	2.5	1.1	9.1	80/90	18	86 (81-91)	8-3
Spatial Relations	61-D	3.7	1.0	9.7	84/90	34	94 (90-98)	8-9
Sound Blending	20	6.8	2.7	11.9	91/90	54	101 (96-107)	11-11
Concept Formation	20-E	3.1	2.1	4.6	60/90	22	89 (85-92)	8-6
Visual Matching	42-2	5.8	4.9	7.0	86/90	44	98 (93-102)	11-1
Numbers Reversed	6	1.0	K.5	1.6	5/90	2	68 (61-74)	6-1
Incomplete Words	26	13.1	5.0	>18.0	96/90	82	114 (107-121)	27
Auditory Work Memory	13	2.9	1.7	4.4	54/90	14	84 (79-88)	8-6
General Information	-	5.8	4.2	7.9	87/90	45	98 (93-103)	11-2
Retrieval Fluency	56	4.4	K.4	>18.0	88/90	31	93 (87-99)	10-1
Picture Recognition	48-D	6.1	2.2	>18.0	90/90	49	100 (95-105)	11-6
Auditory Attention	32	1.7	K.4	7.6	78/90	20	88 (82-93)	7-7
Analysis-Synthesis	20-D	3.2	2.0	5.5	70/90	21	88 (83-93)	8-6
Decision Speed	36	10.3	7.5	>18.0	98/90	86	116 (111-122)	15-2

(continued)

Table 7.2 (Continued)

CLUSTER/Test	RAW	GE	EASY	to DIFF	RPI	PR	SS (68% BAND)	AE
Memory for Words	18	10.4	6.9	>18.0	97/90	71	108 (101-116)	17-6
Rapid Picture Naming	87	2.4	1.5	3.5	27/90	12	83 (81-85)	7-7
Planning	-	5.1	<K.0	>18.0	90/90	44	98 (87-108)	10-2
Pair Cancellation	51	4.0	2.8	5.4	65/90	20	87 (85-89)	9-5
Form B Achievement Tests Administered								
Letter-Word Identification	46	3.6	3.2	4.2	22/90	14	84 (81-86)	8-11
Reading Fluency	43	5.0	4.2	5.9	67/90	33	94 (91-96)	10-5
Story Recall	-	4.8	K.8	>18.0	88/90	39	96 (87-105)	10-3
Understanding Directions	-	3.7	1.9	7.0	78/90	26	90 (86-95)	9-1
Calculation	10	2.5	2.0	3.1	10/90	1	65 (60-71)	7-10
Math Fluency	44	3.3	1.4	5.6	69/90	8	79 (76-81)	8-9
Spelling	25	2.6	2.1	3.3	14/90	5	75 (71-79)	8-0
Writing Fluency	13	3.9	3.0	4.9	50/90	15	85 (81-89)	9-4
Passage Comprehension	26	3.2	2.5	4.4	55/90	15	84 (80-89)	8-6
Applied Problems	33	4.2	3.4	5.1	51/90	22	88 (85-92)	9-9
Writing Samples	6-C	1.9	1.4	3.4	59/90	1	63 (53-73)	7-7
Word Attack	13	2.6	2.1	3.6	36/90	18	86 (84-89)	8-1
Picture Vocabulary	27	6.6	4.6	9.0	92/90	54	102 (97-107)	12-2
Oral Comprehension	22	7.7	4.9	11.4	94/90	61	104 (99-109)	12-5
Editing	7	2.8	2.2	3.5	24/90	6	77 (73-81)	8-0
Reading Vocabulary	-	4.0	2.7	5.8	70/90	25	90 (87-93)	9-5
Quantitative Concepts	-	2.6	1.9	3.3	15/90	3	71 (67-76)	7-11
Academic Knowledge	-	5.1	3.6	6.7	81/90	34	94 (89-98)	10-2
Spelling of Sounds	30	4.4	2.2	8.6	84/90	35	94 (90-98)	9-8
Sound Awareness	34	3.0	2.0	5.3	71/90	21	88 (83-92)	8-8
Punctuation & Capitals	11	2.1	1.5	2.8	16/90	1	63 (55-71)	7-6

| | STANDARD SCORES | | | DISCREPANCY | | Significant at |
DISCREPANCIES	Actual	Predicted	Difference	PR	SD	+ or −1.50 SD (SEE)
Intra-Individual						
COMP-KNOWLEDGE (Gc)	93	85	+8	78	+0.77	No
L-T RETRIEVAL (Glr)	86	88	−2	43	−0.17	No
VIS-SPATIAL THINK (Gv)	96	93	+3	58	+0.19	No
AUDITORY PROCESS (Ga)	95	91	+4	61	+0.28	No
FLUID REASONING (Gf)	87	88	−1	47	−0.06	No
PROCESS SPEED (Gs)	106	91	+15	88	+1.15	No
SHORT-TERM MEM (Gsm)	86	90	−4	37	−0.33	No
PHONEMIC AWARE	108	90	+18	91	+1.36	No
WORKING MEMORY	71	90	−19	5	−1.63	Yes
BASIC READING SKILLS	85	87	−2	41	−0.24	No
READING COMP	85	88	−3	40	−0.26	No
MATH CALC SKILLS	66	91	−25	2	−1.99	Yes
MATH REASONING	80	87	−7	21	−0.81	No
BASIC WRITING SKILLS	74	89	−15	9	−1.36	No
WRITTEN EXPRESSION	78	90	−12	17	−0.96	No
ORAL EXPRESSION	100	88	+12	85	+1.05	No
LISTENING COMP	98	87	+11	84	+0.99	No
ACADEMIC KNOWLEDGE	94	88	+6	73	+0.60	No

(continued)

Table 7.2 (Continued)

DISCREPANCIES	STANDARD SCORES			DISCREPANCY		Significant at
	Actual	Predicted	Difference	PR	SD	+ or −1.50 SD (SEE)
Intellectual Ability/Achievement Discrepancies[1]						
BROAD READING	86	93	−7	23	−0.73	No
BASIC READING SKILLS	85	95	−10	18	−0.92	No
READING COMP	85	94	−9	19	−0.87	No
BROAD MATH	76	95	−19	3	−1.82	Yes
MATH CALC SKILLS	66	96	−30	1	−2.29	Yes
MATH REASONING	80	94	−14	7	−1.45	No
BROAD WRITTEN LANG	74	95	−21	3	−1.87	Yes
BASIC WRITING SKILLS	74	94	−20	4	−1.77	Yes
WRITTEN EXPRESSION	78	94	−16	8	−1.42	No
ORAL LANGUAGE (Ext)	99	94	+5	68	+0.48	No
ORAL EXPRESSION	100	95	+5	69	+0.50	No
LISTENING COMP	98	94	+4	62	+0.31	No
ACADEMIC KNOWLEDGE	94	94	0	50	0.00	No

Note: Norms based on grade 6.2.

[1]These discrepancies based on GIA (Ext) with ACH Broad, Basic, and Applied clusters.

Term Retrieval (*Glr*) reflects her ability to store information efficiently and retrieve it later through association. Kayla's overall ability within this domain (SS = 86 [81-90]) is classified as Low Average, and is within the normal limits of functioning compared to that of same-age peers. Although Kayla demonstrated some difficulty when required to learn and recall a series of rebuses (pictographic representations of words), she was able to rapidly produce a series of words related to specific conditions (e.g., things to eat or drink, first names of people, animals). These results notwithstanding, Kayla's fluency appears to be related to the specific conditions present at the time of retrieval. That is, when Kayla was required to rapidly produce names for a set of narrowly defined concepts, her performance was significantly lower, suggesting that her retrieval is hampered when she must provide responses within a narrowly defined parameter (e.g., when required to say "house" or "home" after being shown a structure resembling a house) as opposed to a broader parameter (e.g., when required to name as many animals as possible). This specific fluency of retrieval difficulty may present itself in other academic areas (e.g., written expression) and may affect the depth and breadth of her vocabulary, resulting in poor-quality writing with limited content.

Visual-Spatial Thinking (*Gv*). Kayla's performance in the area of Visual-Spatial Thinking (*Gv*) suggests that her ability to analyze and synthesize visual stimuli and to hold and manipulate mental images is average (Visual-Spatial Thinking; SS = 96 [92-100]). Kayla was able to adequately identify two or three pieces that formed a complete target shape as well as recognize a subset of previously presented pictures within a field of distracting pictures. Additionally, Kayla demonstrated average ability to use forethought to determine, select, and apply solutions to visually based problems relative to the ability of same-age peers. Kayla's overall performance suggests that her ability to perceive, retain, and manipulate visual patterns is average compared to that of same-age peers. Because Kayla's visual-spatial thinking abilities are classified as Average, teaching her how to rely on visual strategies when learning may prove beneficial. For instance, Kayla could be taught how to visualize an orthographic representation of a word prior to spelling it.

Auditory Processing (*Ga*). Similar to her visual-spatial thinking ability, Kayla's ability to discriminate, analyze, and synthesize auditory stimuli was within normal limits (Auditory Processing; SS = 95 [90-100]; Average). Kayla's ability to blend syllabic and phonemic sounds into whole words and her ability to identify a word with one or more phonemes missing was average. However, when she was required to identify or discriminate sounds under conditions of increasing background noise, her performance was somewhat lower. Kayla's overall ability within this domain will likely serve to benefit her performance in specific academic domains, particularly reading and spelling.

Fluid Reasoning (*Gf*). Kayla's performance in the area of Fluid Reasoning (*Gf*) reflects her ability to reason and solve problems that involve unfamiliar information or procedures. *Gf* is generally manifested in an individual's ability to reorganize, transform, and use information. Kayla's ability to derive rules for a set of presented stimulus items as well as identify the missing parts of an incomplete logic puzzle were average compared to the abilities of same-age peers. Kayla's performance in this domain (Fluid Reasoning; SS = 87 [84-90]; Low Average) suggests that her ability to utilize categorical reasoning based on principles of inductive logic and reason and to draw conclusions from given conditions is within normal limits. Despite Kayla's average performance within this domain, an analysis of her responses revealed that although she was able to adequately identify rules relating to an item's inclusion in a specific category (e.g., all red shapes are included in a set), she demonstrated some difficulty when the number of rules increased (e.g., all little, red, or square shapes are included in a set). This difficulty may be related to Kayla's working memory limitations (described later) and may indicate that Kayla's ability to demonstrate inductive reasoning is affected by the amount of information with which she is required to reason.

Overall Thinking Ability. Based on Kayla's performance in the domains of *Glr, Gv, Ga,* and *Gf,* she obtained a Thinking Ability cluster score of 90 (87-92), which is ranked at the 25th percentile and classified as Average. Her overall performance across these domains suggests that she should be able to acquire sufficient knowledge to perform adequately, in comparison to same-age peers, in a variety of environments (particularly academic). However, on measures of acquired knowledge, Kayla demonstrated variable performance. That is, although her general store of acquired knowledge (*Gc*) and broad reading skills are average compared to those of same-age peers, her knowledge in other domains (math and writing) was very limited.

Cognitive Efficiency

Kayla's cognitive efficiency, or her overall capacity to hold information in conscious awareness and to perform automatic tasks rapidly, is described in the following sections.

Processing Speed (*Gs*). Kayla's performance in the area of Processing Speed (*Gs*) reflects the speed and efficiency with which she can perform automatic or very simple cognitive tasks. Although Kayla demonstrated average ability in terms of visual symbol discrimination, or perceptual speed, the proficiency with which she processed simple concepts and made correct conceptual decisions is advanced. Kayla's overall ability in this domain (Processing Speed; SS = 106 [102-110]; Average), suggests that her ability to efficiently perform simple tasks exceeds that of 66% of her same-age peers.

Short-Term Memory (*Gsm*). Kayla's performance in the area of Short-Term Memory (*Gsm*) reflects her ability to hold information in immediate awareness and then use it within a few seconds. Although Kayla's ability to repeat lists of unrelated words in the correct sequence was average, her ability to repeat a list of numbers in reverse sequence was very limited. Kayla also demonstrated some difficulty when required to reorder a series of digits and words (e.g., 1, apple, 6, shoe, 2) so that the objects were repeated sequentially, followed by the digits. Although Kayla's performance within this domain (Short-Term Memory; SS = 86 [80-92]; Low Average) is estimated to be within normal limits, her limited working memory capacity (Working Memory; SS = 71 [66-75]; Low) likely contributes to her difficulties in math and writing. Specifically, although Kayla is able to retain information in immediate awareness, her performance was mildly impaired when she was required to transform that information in some way (e.g., performing mathematical computations requiring regrouping).

Assessment of Academic Achievement

Results of the WJ III ACH indicate that Kayla's overall performance across the academic domains of reading, math, writing, and oral language is in the low end of Average when compared to that of same-age peers. A detailed review of Kayla's performance appears in the following sections.

Reading

Kayla's performance in the area of reading reflects her ability to identify words, read fluently, and comprehend written text. Kayla's reading ability was assessed through tasks that required her to identify a series of letters and words presented in isolation, read a series of simple sentences and decide whether the statements were true or false, and provide a missing key word that made sense in the context of a previously read passage. Kayla obtained a Broad Reading

DON'T FORGET

The WJ III provides for interpretation at four levels, each of which provides important information about the individual's performance from a unique perspective. In your report, you should include information from all four levels. Your clinical experience will assist you in providing a qualitative interpretation of the individual's performance on the tests. You should also provide information about the individual's level of development, particularly for the academic areas. Developmental information is provided in the form of age or grade equivalents (AEs or GEs) and the developmental bands or instructional ranges. The individual's proficiency with the tasks can best be described by using an interpretation based on the Relative Proficiency Index (RPI). Standard scores (SSs) and percentile ranks (PRs) provide information about relative standing in comparison to same-age or same-grade peers.

cluster score of 86 (84-88), which is ranked at the 18th percentile and classified as Low Average. Kayla's performance within this domain suggests that her reading decoding, reading speed, and ability to comprehend connected discourse while reading is comparable to the average individual in grade 4.0. Consequently, the fifth-grade-level reading tasks in Kayla's current program of instruction are quite difficult for her. Kayla's ability to apply structural and phonic analysis to the pronunciation of unfamiliar printed words is limited. Her ability to read words and supply appropriate meanings is average. Her average performance notwithstanding, an examination of Kayla's proficiency in this domain relative to that of same-age peers suggests that although she demonstrates average proficiency on reading speed, she has limited proficiency in terms of reading comprehension and word identification as compared to same-grade peers. More specifically, on similar tasks of reading decoding and comprehension, Kayla is predicted to perform with only 29% and 63% success, respectively, those tasks that average age- or grade-mates perform with 90% success.

Mathematics

Kayla's performance on mathematics tasks was variable. On a task requiring her to solve basic computational problems, her performance was limited. Although Kayla demonstrated the ability to add and subtract single- and double-digit numbers fairly accurately, she often confused the operation to be performed. For instance, when computing an addition problem requiring regrouping (e.g., "15 + 6"), Kayla subtracted the numbers. Similarly, when problems required two numbers to be multiplied (e.g., "8 × 7"), Kayla calculated the difference between the two. Thus, although her responses to the operations she performed were accurate, her facility with basic operational symbols was not. Kayla demonstrated a similar limitation on a task requiring her to quickly add, subtract, and multiply a series of single-digit numbers. Although she self-corrected at times, she again evidenced difficulty with the specific operation required (i.e., calculated "4 − 3" as "7" and "1 + 1" as "0"). Additionally, Kayla often resorted to counting on her fingers to perform basic operations, which further served to impair her fluency.

Kayla's performance on the Calculation test was also limited. A review of her responses indicates that Kayla's strategies, rather than her facility with basic math facts, may have enhanced her performance. For instance, when presented with a problem that required her to sum numbers, Kayla counted tally marks that she had made on the Subject Response Booklet to arrive at her response. Moreover, when a problem required the application of more-advanced computational skills (e.g., multiplication), such as "120 × 5," Kayla resorted to a very basic computational strategy (e.g., addition) by restructuring the problem (i.e., she added the number 120 five times). Thus, although Kayla's performance on applied math tasks appears to suggest an understanding of a range of mathematical concepts and operations, it is evident that her strategies, rather than her facility with basic math facts, were responsible for her overall performance.

When asked to demonstrate conceptual understanding that was not amenable to the application of strategies (e.g., when she was asked a direct question regarding her knowledge of a particular concept), Kayla's performance was lower. For instance, Kayla was unable to identify the operation required by a specific sign (e.g., multiplication) and she could not provide the appropriate labels for numbers that exceeded the hundredths place value (e.g., 1,200). Overall, Kayla's performance in the area of math (Broad Math, SS = 76 [73-79]; Low) is comparable to that of the average individual in grade 3.3 and suggests that her current fourth-grade-level instruction in mathematics is too difficult for her. Kayla's proficiency with basic math facts is particularly lacking. Specifically, on tasks requiring her to perform basic math computations, Kayla is predicted to perform with only 10% success on computational tasks that average age- or grade-mates perform with 90% success.

DON'T FORGET

The Age/Grade Profile provides a graphic portrayal of WJ III results. This profile is particularly useful in communicating developmental or instructional level information to teachers and parents. With the Age/Grade Profile, teachers and parents can easily see if the student's current level of instruction falls within limits that would not be either too easy or too difficult for the student. The Age/Grade Profile will be a useful supplement to a written report.

Written Language

Kayla's performance in the area of writing (Broad Written Language, SS = 74 [71-78]; Low) is low. Her spelling ability, fluency of written production, and quality of written expression are comparable to those of the average individual in grade 2.9. As in the area of math, Kayla's performance within this academic domain suggests that she has basic skill deficits that impede her writing ability. When compared to same-aged peers, Kayla demonstrated low performance when required to spell a series of words presented in isolation. Although Kayla was able to rely on her knowledge of sound/symbol associations, which facilitated performance on phonetic spelling tasks, her over-reliance on the phonetic representations of words (e.g., spelled "laughing" as "lafing" and "juice" as "juies"), served to moderately impair her overall spelling performance. For example, Kayla's ability to recall how common words look or to spell words with silent sounds was very limited (e.g., spelled "comb" as "com" and "before" as "befor"). Fourth-grade-level tasks (the level at which she is currently receiving instruction) involving written language will be too difficult for her. Her expected proficiency on similar tasks of spelling suggests that she will be able to perform with only 14% success on tasks that her average age- and grade-mates perform with 90% success.

Kayla also demonstrated difficulty on other tasks of basic writing skills. Specifically, her ability to correct errors in spelling, punctuation, capitalization, and word usage is limited. Her ability to use punctuation and capitalization skills appropriately when presented with dictated sentences is very limited. In addition, Kayla demonstrated a limited ability to generate written text. That is, when she was required to generate sentences in response to picture prompts (e.g., a picture of a cow eating grass), Kayla merely labeled the picture ("a cow") and failed to produce complete sentences. Similarly, when presented with a picture of a man waving to someone passing in a car, Kayla wrote "a man waving to a car." Her performance suggests that in addition to basic skill deficits, Kayla has not acquired a solid understanding of the basic sentence structure required to generate complete sentences. However, when Kayla was provided with the requisite components of a sentence, her performance improved. For instance, when presented with a picture of a clock and the words "clock," "not," and "working," Kayla produced the sentence, "the clock is not working." Kayla's performance suggests that she can benefit from added structure and context when presented with writing tasks.

Oral Language

Kayla's expressive oral language skills (and receptive language abilities) are commensurate with those of same-age peers (Oral Language; SS = 99 [96-102]; Average). Expressively, Kayla demonstrated the ability to recall details from a series of increasingly complex stories and provide labels for a series of pictured objects. Receptively, Kayla was able to listen and respond to a series of directions requiring her to point to individual objects embedded in a larger scene as well as use syntactic and semantic cues to supply an appropriate missing key word from an orally presented passage. Overall, Kayla's performance in this domain suggests that her expressive and receptive oral language skills are well within normal limits. In terms of her relative proficiency, Kayla's performance on tasks of listening comprehension suggests that she would be predicted to demonstrate 88% proficiency with similar tasks that average age- and grade-mates would also perform with 90% proficiency. Finally, in terms of Oral Expression, Kayla is predicted to perform with 90% success those tasks that average age- or grade-mates perform with 90% success.

Kayla's math calculation, written expression, and basic writing skills are comparable to those of the average student in grade 2.7. As seen in Table 7.2, academic tasks of math calculation and written expression that are commensurate with end-of-first-grade work will be quite easy for Kayla, as will academic tasks involving basic writing skills that are commensurate with a beginning second-grade level. Kayla's performance in the areas of math reasoning, basic reading skills, and reading comprehension is comparable to that of the average student in third grade; thus, tasks within these areas that are commensurate with end-of-second-grade work will be easy for Kayla. Despite her low instructional levels in the aforementioned areas, Kayla is performing near or at grade level in the area of listening comprehension and oral expression. More specifically, Kayla's performance in these domains is comparable to that of the average student in fifth and sixth grades, respectively. In designing instructional materials for Kayla, teachers should bear in mind that she will be most appropriately challenged in the areas of math calculation and basic writing skills if such tasks are commensurate with a mid-third-grade level. Similarly, Kayla should be presented with tasks commensurate with a beginning fourth-grade level in the areas of basic reading, math reasoning, and written expression. Although Kayla's performance in the majority of academic areas suggests a third- to fourth-grade ability level, she demonstrates the ability to handle fifth-grade material for tasks of reading comprehension.

Data Integration and Interpretation

Data obtained from the administration of the WJ III COG and WJ III ACH tests indicate that Kayla's abilities range from Low to High Average. In terms of cognitive performance, Kayla's ability to quickly process relatively simple stimuli (*Gs*) is high average, whereas her vocabulary knowledge and ability to reason with lexical information are average. Similarly, her ability to analyze and synthesize auditory and visual stimuli (i.e., *Ga, Gv*) is average. However, Kayla's overall abilities to retain and transform information (*Gsm*); to reason using novel procedures (*Gf*); and to encode, transfer, and consolidate information (*Glr*) into her general fund of acquired knowledge, and later retrieve that knowledge, are low average.

Although Kayla's overall cognitive performance suggests that she should be able to learn, acquire new information, and demonstrate such knowledge in academic areas (e.g., reading, writing, and math), her academic performance does not consistently reflect this. Although Kayla's oral language abilities are average and her math reasoning and reading abilities are within normal limits (i.e., low average), her basic math calculation skills, writing skills, and written expression are very limited to limited and she cannot perform these basic skills automatically. The differences between Kayla's abilities within and across these academic domains is best understood by examining the relationship between specific cognitive abilities and academic achievement areas as well as analyzing Kayla's performance within the context of an *Information Processing Model* (IPM; see Figure 7.1). Although it seems clear that Kayla's specific cognitive weaknesses (especially working memory and naming facility) are related

Name __Kayla__   Sex __F__   Age __11__   Grade __6__

Examiner __Bob Johnson__   Date __11/07/00__

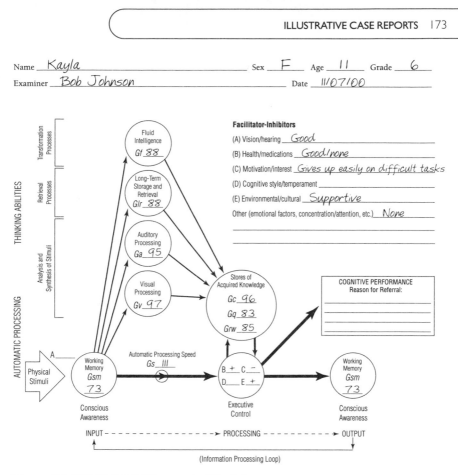

Figure 7.1 WJ III COG Diagnostic Worksheet

Source: Adapted from *WJ III Tests of Cognitive Abilities Examiner's Manual*, p. 83, Riverside Publishing 2001.

to her academic skills deficits, a more complete understanding of how Kayla's individual pattern of strengths and weaknesses interact to affect her real-world performance (e.g., her academic functioning) can be gleaned from analyzing them within the context of the IPM. Moreover, this type of analysis allows for predictions regarding Kayla's performance across varying task demands and conditions.

As indicated in Figure 7.1, Kayla demonstrated considerable variability in terms of her stores of acquired knowledge. Although her Comprehension-Knowledge score (*Gc*) was average, her Quantitative Knowledge score (*Gq*) and her Reading and Writing (*Grw*) ability, based on her broad reading and written language performance, were low average. With regard to academic functioning, Kayla's average abilities in the areas of Comprehension-Knowledge (*Gc*) partly explain her average performance on receptive and expressive oral language tasks as well as on tasks requiring reading. Conversely, her overall low to low-average scores in *specific* aspects of writing ability and quantitative knowledge partly explain her reported difficulties with classroom tasks requiring the application of such knowledge.

In terms of oral language, although Kayla's comprehension and production of language are dependent on a number of factors, her average language development, lexical knowledge, general fund of information, and listening ability (all of which are *Gc* abilities) contribute to her solid ability to use and comprehend spoken language. Kayla's ability in this domain suggests that she ought to be able to participate in, and benefit from, activities involving the comprehension or production of spoken language (e.g., giving oral reports in class, listening to a class lecture). Given that Kayla has an adequate fund of verbally based information, she is able to draw upon her *Gc* abilities to facilitate new learning. Additionally, if Kayla is presented with information that is not readily available in this knowledge store (e.g., a new vocabulary word), she is able to utilize her intact thinking abilities in an attempt to produce a response. For instance, Kayla may utilize her visual or auditory processing abilities in an effort to define a word, perhaps trying to find a familiar word that sounds similar to the new word before defining it, or visualizing where she has seen the word used in a prior context.

Although Kayla's overall average performance in the area of reading is partly explained by her sufficient fund of acquired verbal knowledge (*Gc*), her performance is also explained by her ability in other cognitive domains (e.g., *Grw, Ga, Glr, Gs, Gv*). In terms of their relationship to reading, *Gc* abilities such as language development, lexical knowledge, and general information are primarily related to reading comprehension. Thus, when Kayla is required to comprehend written text, her vocabulary skills and fund of prior knowledge facilitate her performance. Similarly, although Kayla's overall reading and writing ability (*Grw*), based on her broad reading and written language performance, was estimated in the Low Average range, the particular abilities related to reading (reading decoding, reading speed) were within normal limits. Thus Kayla can draw upon these abilities when she is required to decode written text. Moreover, although Kayla demonstrates an over-reliance on phonetic strategies in decoding words, her ability in this domain seems to have provided her with some success in terms of basic reading skills. Additionally, although Kayla's weaknesses in rapid automatic naming may suggest some difficulty in retrieving labels for particular words she encounters, her perceptual speed (a Gs ability), coupled with her reliance on context, appears to allow her to compensate for this deficit as it relates to tasks involving reading.

Although Kayla's range of acquired verbal knowledge (Gc) facilitates success in the areas of reading and oral language, such knowledge is insufficient to ensure success in other academic areas, particularly writing and mathematics. For instance, although Kayla has sufficient vocabulary and background knowledge (Gc) to generate ideas, her knowledge of basic writing skills is limited and therefore interferes with her ability to appropriately organize and express her thoughts in writing. Thus, although Kayla's ability to rely on her stores of knowledge to generate ideas could serve to enhance the quality of the content of her writing, the structure of her writing is hindered by her lack of automaticity in basic writing skills and her very limited knowledge of grammatical structures, syntax, and basic mechanics (e.g., punctuation and capitalization). As task demands increase (i.e., coherence and fluency are emphasized), Kayla demonstrates additional difficulty and her performance becomes highly dependent on the context available to her (e.g., visual cues and specific words to be used in a sentence). Overall, it appears that Kayla's relevant store of acquired reading and writing knowledge (Grw) is too limited to allow her to generate written, connected text independently. Moreover, although it is quite possible for Kayla to use her intact thinking abilities, such as Fluid Reasoning, to aid her in some elements of the writing process (e.g., generating creative ideas), use of such abilities will be constrained in the absence of interventions designed to improve her knowledge and skills of basic writing. It is important to note that even when Kayla is able to utilize her thinking abilities (e.g., Ga) to aid in her basic writing skills, such as spelling, she often demonstrates an over-reliance on such skills (e.g., phonics), which subsequently serves to limit her achievement.

Although Kayla's store of quantitative knowledge appears relatively stronger than her acquired knowledge in writing, she still experiences a mild delay in this academic domain. That is, although Kayla demonstrated average ability in applied mathematics reasoning, her performance was largely aided by the application of rudimentary strategies. Therefore, these scores may represent an overestimate of her quantitative reasoning abilities. Kayla's limited fund of quantitative concepts further supports this hypothesis. Specifically, when Kayla is required to provide information in regard to her conceptual knowledge of mathematics that is not amenable to strategy use, her performance is significantly impaired. Although Kayla can rely on her relevant store of acquired knowledge (*Gq*) in attempting mathematical tasks, her depth and breadth of knowledge in this domain are insufficient to facilitate skilled performance. Thus, she seems to over-rely on a select set of basic strategies. Although such strategy use is understandable because it has brought her relative success in computations and problems that are amenable to such strategies, it is inefficient. Moreover, continued reliance on such strategies appears to have precluded Kayla from attempting to generate different mechanisms to strengthen her basic skills in this domain.

Overall, an examination of Kayla's abilities suggests that she has specific academic delays, and has not acquired the level of automaticity in math and writing that is necessary to facilitate new learning. The absence of basic foundational skills in math and writing hinders Kayla's ability to demonstrate success in these areas. Kayla's basic math and writing skill limitations lead to an overreliance on fundamental strategies or to inefficient strategy use. Although Kayla's thinking abilities are intact, her executive processes (Executive Processes; SS = 85 [83-88]) are low average when compared to those of other individuals her age. Consequently, she may not be particularly adept at formulating and employing strategies to acquire new knowledge. Additionally, it appears that her limited range of strategies and her reliance on rudimentary strategies constrains the development of existing skills and the acquisition of new skills that would provide her with better information to develop more effective strategies. This bi-directional relationship between executive processes and the acquisition of knowledge is further affected by Kayla's limited working-memory capacity. Kayla demonstrated a limitation in working memory processes, specifically when she was required to segment and transform sets of information.

To summarize, Kayla's cognitive and academic limitations appear to be directly related to her reported inability to acquire higher-level reading and math skills. The impact of Kayla's cognitive ability levels on her academic achievement does not appear to be related to external factors such as environmental influences, poor instruction, or other exclusionary factors (e.g., hearing and vision). Kayla's circumscribed patterns of cognitive and academic weaknesses, coupled with her intact functioning in her ability to think, acquire general knowledge, and read, indicate that she has a specific learning disability in the areas of math calculation and written expression.

Recommendations

The evaluation of information provided by standardized tests, teacher and parent reports, qualitative analysis of responses, and prereferral data served as the basis for the following recommendations for Kayla:

1. The grade level at which Kayla is currently receiving instruction in mathematics and writing is too difficult for her. When expected to perform independently with math and writing activities that are too difficult for her, Kayla becomes withdrawn and inattentive. Consequently, she should receive an individualized educational program (IEP) in these areas through the learning disabilities (LD) program offered at Jefferson Elementary. In addition to the development of an individually tailored program, the LD educational consultant should work with Kayla's mother to provide her with information that will enable her to reinforce Kayla's program goals within the home environment.

2. Kayla's working memory deficit is related to her difficulties in math and writing. To aid Kayla in educational activities that require the retention and manipulation of information, teachers should use memory strategies and techniques (for instance, academic tasks can be sequenced from simple to complex). Additionally, given that Kayla's short-term memory, in terms of memory span, is sufficient, she should be able to memorize basic facts (e.g., multiplication tables). Kayla's teacher can provide her with frequent opportunities for practice and review.

3. Kayla's current strategy use is related to her lack of automaticity in the areas of math and writing. Kayla should be taught effective and efficient strategies that she can practice and ultimately apply in these academic domains.

4. Analysis of Kayla's responses revealed that she lacks basic math

skills, which affects her computational and numerical reasoning abilities. Thus, intervention should focus on skill building (i.e., engaging Kayla in tasks and activities that will allow her to master basic skills). Basic skills in the area of math can be taught and or reinforced by (a) providing Kayla with manipulatives (e.g., base-10 blocks) to reinforce the concept of regrouping; (b) teaching Kayla relevant vocabulary often found in math problems that indicate specific operations (e.g., together, sum, in all, difference, between, less, times, product, average, half as many); (c) highlighting or underlining key words in math problems (e.g., the reference to the operation involved); and (d) providing Kayla with a checklist to follow in solving math problems (e.g., what information is given, what question is asked, what operation is used).

5. Although Kayla demonstrates the application of sound-symbol correspondence when presented with spelling tasks, she tends to over-rely on such strategies. Given that her spelling errors reflect reasonable phonic alternatives, however, her prognosis in terms of increasing basic spelling skills is good. Therefore, remedial efforts should focus on teaching Kayla orthographic relationships. This could be accomplished by introducing her to visually based spelling strategies, such as a cover-copy-compare technique. Such a technique would allow Kayla to look at a word, attempt to write it from memory, and check her accuracy. A tracing component could be added to further aid retention and Kayla could copy all learned words in a notebook to be used for review.

6. Kayla's difficulty in basic writing skills, such as editing, can be addressed in natural writing situations. One useful strategy may be to provide Kayla with an individualized proofreading checklist that she can use prior to submitting written work (e.g., Does each sentence begin with a capital? Does every sentence end with a period?, etc.). In terms of addressing usage errors, Kayla can be asked to read her writing aloud so that she can listen for any inconsistencies in the text flow. Identification of such inconsistencies can serve to cue her to the particular location of the error.

7. To address Kayla's difficulties in constructing complete sentences, she can be provided with an adapted sentence-guide method that

teaches generation, elaboration, and ordering of sentence elements. For instance, Kayla can be provided with a cueing card that reads "Who? What doing? To whom?" or "Who? What doing? When? Where? Why?" Such questions may refer to a picture or a written story. After answering the questions, Kayla can attempt to write a complete sentence. For instance, if shown a picture of a boy tossing a Frisbee to a dog, Kayla's answers to the "Who? What doing? To whom?" sequence would likely be "the boy, tossing a Frisbee, to the dog." Adding a simple sentence element (i.e., the verb "is") would allow Kayla to form a complete sentence (i.e., "The boy is tossing a Frisbee to the dog."). As Kayla's skill in generating sentences and elaborating on them develops, the order of the presented questions may be modified.

8. Other recommendations for teaching and reinforcing basic writing skills should focus on (a) providing Kayla with direct instruction and practice relating to the rules of capitalization (e.g., first word of a sentence, the pronoun "I," proper names, months, holidays, states, streets, book titles, etc.) and punctuation (e.g., a period belongs at the end of a sentence, a question mark is used when a question is asked, etc.); (b) teaching Kayla the parts of a sentence and having her practice constructing sentences from a series of controlled word lists; (c) providing Kayla the opportunity to correct her own work by giving her a key that highlights the types of errors she committed (e.g., one missing comma, two capitalization errors) and allowing her to attempt to identify the location of her error; and (d) attempting to organize writing tasks by having Kayla dictate her thoughts and ideas into a tape recorder and later transcribe her words into a written essay.

References

Alloy, L. B., Acocella, J., & Bootzin, R. R. (1996). *Abnormal psychology: Current perspectives* (7th ed.). New York: McGraw-Hill.

American Educational Research Association (AERA), American Psychological Association (APA), & National Council on Measurement in Education (NCME). (1999). *Standards for educational and psychological testing.* Washington, DC: AERA.

Betts, E. (1957). *Foundations of reading instruction* (2nd ed.). New York: American Book.

Borkowski, J. G., & Burke, J. E. (1996). Theories, models, and measurements of executive functioning: An information processing perspective. In G. R. Lyon & N. A. Krasnegor (Eds.), *Attention, memory, and executive function* (pp. 235–262). Baltimore, MD: Brookes.

Brackett, J., & McPherson, A. (1996). Learning disabilities diagnosis in postsecondary students: A comparison of discrepancy-based diagnostic models. In N. Gregg, C. Hoy, & A. F. Gay (Eds.), *Adults with learning disabilities: Theoretical and practical perspectives* (pp. 68–84). New York: Guilford.

Carroll, J. B. (1983). Studying individual differences in cognitive abilities: Through and beyond factor analysis. In R. F. Dillon (Ed.), *Individual differences in cognition* (Vol. 1, pp. 1–33). New York: Academic Press.

Carroll, J. B. (1993). *Human cognitive abilities: A survey of factor-analytic studies.* New York: Cambridge University Press.

Carroll, J. B. (1998). Human cognitive abilities: A critique. In J. J. McArdle & R. W. Woodcock (Eds.), *Human cognitive abilities in theory and practice* (pp. 5–24). Mahwah, NJ: Erlbaum.

Cattell, R. B. (1941). Some theoretical issues in adult intelligence testing. *Psychological Bulletin, 38,* 592.

Denckla, M. B. (1989). Executive function, the overlap zone between Attention Deficit Hyperactivity Disorder and learning disabilities. *International Pediatrics, 4,* 155–160.

Ekstrom, R. B., French, J. W., & Harman, M. H. (1979). Cognitive factors: Their identification and replication. *Multivariate Behavioral Research Monographs, 79*(2).

Elliott, C. D. (1990). Differential Ability Scales. San Antonio, TX: Psychological Corporation.

Flanagan, D. P., Berneir, J., Keiser, S., & Ortiz, S. (2001). Diagnosing learning disability in adulthood. Manuscript submitted for publication.

Flanagan, D. P., McGrew, K. S., & Ortiz, S. O. (2000). *The Wechsler intelligence scales and Gf-Gc theory: A contemporary approach to interpretation.* Boston: Allyn & Bacon.

Flanagan, D. P., Ortiz, S. O., Alfonso, V. C., & Mascolo, J. T. (2002). *The achievement test desk reference: Comprehensive assessment and learning disability.* Boston: Allyn & Bacon.

Fletcher, J. M., Francis, D. J., Shaywitz, S. E., Lyon, G. R., Foorman, B. R., Stuebing, K. K., & Shaywitz, B. A. (1998). Intelligent testing and the discrepancy model for children with learning disabilities. *Learning Disabilities Research and Practice, 13,* 186–203.

Galton, F. (1869). *Hereditary genius: An enquiry into its laws and consequences.* London: Collins.

Hidi, S. (1990). Interest and its contribution as a mental resource for learning. *Review of Educational Research, 60,* 549–571.

Horn, J. L. (1965). *Fluid and crystallized intelligence.* Unpublished doctoral dissertation, University of Illinois, Urbana-Champaign.

Horn, J. L. (1991). Measurement of intellectual capabilities: A review of theory. In K. S. McGrew, J. K. Werder, and R. W. Woodcock, *WJ-R Technical Manual* (pp. 197–232). Itasca, IL: Riverside.

Horn, J. L., & Noll, J. (1997). Human cognitive capabilities: *Gf-Gc* theory. In D. P. Flanagan, J. L. Genshaft, & P. L. Harrison (Eds.), *Contemporary intellectual assessment: Theories, tests, and issues* (pp. 53–91). New York: Guilford.

Jensen, A. R. (1998). *The g factor.* Westport, CT: Praeger.

Lyon, R. G., Fletcher, J. M., Shaywitz, S. E., Shaywitz, B. A., Torgesen, J. K., Wood, F. B., Schulte, A., & Olson, R. (2001). Rethinking learning disabilities. In C. E. Finn, A. J. Rotherham, & C. R. Hokanson, Jr. (Eds.), *Rethinking special education for a new century.* Dayton, Ohio: Thomas B. Fordham Foundation.

Mather, N., & Schrank, F. A. (2001). Use of the WJ III Discrepancy Procedures for Learning Disabilities Identification and Diagnosis (Assessment Service Bulletin No. 3). Itasca, IL: Riverside.

Mather, N., Wendling, B. J., & Woodcock, R. W. (2001). *Essentials of WJ III Tests of Achievement Assessment.* New York: Wiley.

Mather, N., & Woodcock, R. W. (2001). Examiner's Manual. *Woodcock-Johnson III Tests of Cognitive Abilities.* Itasca, IL: Riverside.

McGrew, K. S., & Flanagan, D. P. (1998). *The intelligence test desk reference (ITDR): Gf-Gc Cross-Battery Assessment.* Boston: Allyn & Bacon.

McGrew, K. S., Werder, J. K., & Woodcock, R. W. (1991). *WJ-R technical manual.* Itasca, IL: Riverside.

McGrew, K. S., & Woodcock, R. W. (2001). Woodcock-Johnson III *Technical manual.* Itasca, IL: Riverside.

Messick, S. (1998). Validity of psychological assessment: Validation of inferences from persons' responses and performances as scientific inquiry into score meaning. In A. E. Kazdin (Ed.), *Methodological issues & strategies in clinical research* (2nd ed.) (pp. 241–261). Washington, DC: American Psychological Association.

Naglieri, J. A., and Das, J. P. (1997). Das•Naglieri Cognitive Assessment System. Itasca, IL: Riverside.

Pennington, B. F. (1997). Dimensions of executive functions in normal and abnormal development. In N. A. Krasnegor, G. R. Lyon, & P. S. Goldman-Rakic (Eds.), *Development of the prefrontal cortex: Evolution, neurobiology, and behavior* (pp. 265–281). Baltimore, MD: Brookes.

Rack, J. P., Snowling, M. J., & Olson, R. K. (1992). The nonword reading deficit in developmental dyslexia: A review. *Reading Research Quarterly, 27*(1), 28–53.

Scarborough, H. S. (1991). Antecedents to reading disability: Preschool language development and literacy experiences of children from dyslexic families. In B. F. Pennington (Ed.), *Reading disabilities: Genetic and neurological influences* (pp. 31–45). Dordrecht, The Netherlands: Kluwer.

Schrank, F. A., McGrew, K. S., & Woodcock, R. W. (2001). *Assessment Service Bulletin Number 2: WJ III Technical Abstract.* Itasca, IL: Riverside Publishing.

Schrank, F. A., & Woodcock, R. W. (2001). WJ III Compuscore and Profiles Program [Computer software]. Itasca, IL: Riverside.

Schrank, F. A., & Woodcock, R. W. (2002). Report Writer for the WJ III [Computer software]. *Woodcock-Johnson III.* Itasca, IL: Riverside.

Snow, R. E. (1989a). Aptitude-treatment interaction as a framework for research on individual differences in learning. In P. L. Ackerman & R. J. Sternberg (Eds.), *Learning and individual differences in theory and research* (pp. 13–59). New York: Freeman.

Snow, R. E. (1989b). Cognitive-conative aptitude interactions in learning. In R. Kanfer, P. L. Ackerman, & R. Cudeck (Eds.), *Abilities, motivation, methodology: The Minnesota Symposium on Learning and Individual Differences* (pp. 435–474). Hillsdale, NJ: Erlbaum.

Spearman, C. (1904). General intelligence, objectively determined and measured. *American Journal of Psychology, 15,* 201–293.

Spearman, C. (1927). *The abilities of man: Their nature and measurement.* New York: Macmillan.

Stanovich, K. E. (1991). Discrepancy definitions of reading disability: Has intelligence led us astray? *Reading Research Quarterly, 26*(1), 7–29.

Thorndike, R. L. (1963). *The concepts of over and under achievement.* New York: Columbia University Bureau of Publications.

Thorndike, R. L., Hagen, E. P., & Sattler, J. S. (1986). Stanford-Binet Intelligence Scale, Fourth Edition. Itasca, IL: Riverside.

Torgesen, J. K., Wagner, R. K., Rashotte, C. A., Rose, E., Lindamood, P., Conway, J., & Garvan, C. (1999). Preventing reading failure in young children with phonological processing disabilities: Group and individual responses to instruction. *Journal of Educational Psychology, 91,* 579–594.

U.S. Department of Education. (1999). *Assistance to states for the education of children with disabilities and the early intervention program for infants and toddlers with disabilities.* Final regulations. Washington, DC: Author.

Wechsler, D. (1991). Wechsler Intelligence Scale for Children–Third Edition. San Antonio, TX: Psychological Corporation.

Wechsler, D. (1997). Wechsler Adult Intelligence Scale–Third Edition. San Antonio, TX: Psychological Corporation.

Wertsch, J. (1985). *Vygotsky and the social formation of the mind.* Cambridge, MA: Harvard University Press.

WJ III Newsletter, Vol. 1, Spring 2001. Itasca, IL: Riverside Publishing.

Woodcock, R. W. (1956). Construction and evaluation of a test for predicting success in remedial reading. Unpublished doctoral dissertation, University of Oregon, Eugene.

Woodcock, R. W. (1958). An experimental prognostic test for remedial readers. *Journal of Educational Psychology, 49,* 23–27.

Woodcock, R. W. (1990). Theoretical foundations of the WJ-R measures of cognitive ability. *Journal of Psychoeducational Assessment, 8,* 231–258.

Woodcock, R. W. (1992, April). *Rasch technology and test engineering.* Paper presented at the American Educational Research Association Annual Conference, San Francisco, CA.

Woodcock, R. W. (1993). An information processing view of Gf-Gc theory. *Journal of Psychoeducational Assessment Monograph Series, WJ-R Monograph,* 80–102.

Woodcock, R. W. (1997). *The Woodcock-Johnson Tests of Cognitive Ability—Revised.* In D. P. Flanagan, J. L. Genshaft, & P. L. Harrison (Eds.), *Contemporary intellectual assessment: Theories, tests, and issues* (pp. 230–246). New York: Guilford Press.

Woodcock, R. W., & Johnson, M. B. (1977). Woodcock-Johnson Psycho-Educational Battery. Itasca, IL: Riverside.

Woodcock, R. W., & Johnson, M. B. (1989a). Woodcock-Johnson Psycho-Educational Battery–Revised. Itasca, IL: Riverside.

Woodcock, R. W., & Johnson, M. B. (1989b). WJ-R Tests of Achievement. Itasca, IL: Riverside.

Woodcock, R. W., & Johnson, M. B. (1989c). WJ-R Tests of Cognitive Ability. Itasca, IL: Riverside.

Woodcock, R. W., McGrew, K. S., & Mather, N. (2001a). *Woodcock-Johnson III.* Itasca, IL: Riverside.

Woodcock, R. W., McGrew, K. S., & Mather, N. (2001b). *Woodcock-Johnson III Tests of Achievement.* Itasca, IL: Riverside.

Woodcock, R. W., McGrew, K. S., & Mather, N. (2001c). *Woodcock-Johnson III Tests of Cognitive Abilities.* Itasca, IL: Riverside.

Annotated Bibliography

Carroll, J. B. (1993). *Human cognitive abilities: A survey of factor-analytic studies.* Cambridge: Cambridge University Press.

This seminal work had a significant impact on the design of the WJ III. It reviews approximately 1,500 references covering the last 50–60 years of factor-analytic research. Carroll used exploratory methods, letting the data emerge. This work resulted in Carroll's Three-Stratum Theory of Intelligence. Carroll's work was combined with the work of Raymond Cattell and John Horn to form the CHC theory that underlies the WJ III.

Flanagan, D. P., Ortiz, S. O., Alfonso, V. C., & Mascolo, J. T. (2002). *The Achievement Test Desk Reference (ATDR): Comprehensive assessment and learning disability.* Boston: Allyn & Bacon.

The ATDR provides psychometric, qualitative, and theoretical information for more than 50 recent achievement tests and batteries. In addition, the authors of the ATDR present an operational definition of learning disability (LD) and demonstrate how to use both achievement and cognitive ability tests within a comprehensive framework for LD determination, based on this definition. Numerous tables, charts, summary sheets, and worksheets organized around CHC theory and the seven academic areas of LD listed in the federal definition facilitate comprehensive and selective assessment.

Mather, N. (1991). *An instructional guide to the Woodcock-Johnson Psycho-Educational Battery–Revised.* New York: Wiley.

Although based on the WJ-R, this book provides a wealth of information about instructional strategies and approaches for the academic areas covered in the test; since the WJ III covers the same broad academic areas, the information is still applicable. Various instructional approaches for remediating each academic area are explained, and sample psychoeducational reports are included in the Appendix. The intent of the book is to help examiners who use the WJ-R translate test results into meaningful information for program development. The cognitive tests are included, but the primary focus is on the achievement tests.

Mather, N., & Woodcock, R. W. (2001). Woodcock-Johnson III Tests of Achievement *Examiner's manual.* Itasca, IL: Riverside.

The manual comes as part of the WJ III ACH test kit. It provides a description of the tests and clusters in the WJ III ACH, as well as information about administering, scoring, and interpreting the test. The Scoring Guide for Writing Samples, the Handwriting Legibility Scale, and the reproducible Writing Evaluation Scale are included in the Appendices.

Mather, N., & Jaffe, L. (in press). *Woodcock-Johnson III: Recommendations and reports.* New York: Wiley.

This book is intended to serve as a resource for evaluators using the WJ III in educational and clinical settings. Its purpose is to assist examiners in preparing and writing psychoeducational reports for individuals of all ages. It covers both the cognitive and achievement batteries.

McGrew, K. S., & Woodcock, R. W. (2001). Woodcock-Johnson III *Technical manual.* Itasca, IL: Riverside.

This manual comes as part of the WJ III ACH test kit. It provides information about the design criteria for the complete WJ III, development of the norms, and the standardization procedures. Reliability and validity studies are presented. Both the cognitive and achievement batteries are covered in this manual. Numerous statistical tables are included for clinicians and researchers.

Mather, N., Wendling, B. J., & Woodcock, R. W. (2001). *Essentials of the WJ III Tests of Achievement Assessment.* New York: Wiley.

This is a companion book covering the administration, scoring, and interpretation of the WJ III ACH. For those using the cognitive battery with the WJ III ACH, this book will provide additional insights for interpretation.

Schrank, F. A., & Woodcock, R. W. (2002). *Report Writer for the WJ III.* Itasca, IL: Riverside.

This computer woftware program calculates all scores and produces first-draft reports based on the WJ III interpretive model. The program includes a set of reproducible criterion-referenced checklists to help gather and document contextual information for a comprehensive assessment. The program automates many clerical aspects of WJ III interpretation, such as comparisons of significance between tests that comprise a cluster. Completion of the WJ III Diagnostic Worksheet is also automated.

Index

About the Authors

Fredrick A. Schrank is executive director of the Woodcock-Muñoz Foundation. A licensed psychologist, Dr. Schrank holds the Diplomate in School Psychology from the American Board of Professional Psychology (ABPP) and is a Fellow of the American Academy of School Psychology. He serves on the board of directors of the American Board of School Psychology. Prior to earning his doctorate from the University of Wisconsin-Madison, Dr. Schrank gained a broad background in school psychological services in elementary and secondary schools and colleges and universities. He is the senior author (with Richard W. Woodcock) of the *Report Writer for the WJ III.*

Dawn P. Flanagan is associate professor of psychology at St. John's University, New York. Dr. Flanagan is codeveloper (with Kevin S. McGrew and Samuel O. Ortiz) of the CHC Cross-Battery Approach. She is senior author of the *Wechsler Intelligence Scales and* Gf-Gc *Theory; Essentials of Cross-Battery Assessment;* and *The Achievement Test Desk Reference: A Comprehensive Framework for LD Determination.* Dr. Flanagan is a Fellow of the American Psychological Association and a recipient of this organization's Lightner Witmer Award. She earned her doctorate from the Ohio State University in Columbus.

Richard W. Woodcock is the senior author (with Kevin S. McGrew and Nancy Mather) of the *Woodcock-Johnson III Tests of Cognitive Abilities* and *Tests of Achievement.* Dr. Woodcock has a wide background in education and psychology. He has held a variety of positions, including elementary school teacher, school psychologist, director of special education, and university professor. Most recently (1993–1998), Dr. Woodcock held the title of research professor in the Department of Psychology at the University of Virginia. He earned the doctorate from the University of Oregon.

Jennifer T. Mascolo is a doctoral student at St. John's University, New York. Her research interests include psychological assessment, evaluation, and testing, as well as examining the nature and structure of human cognitive abilities. She is coauthor of *The Achievement Test Desk Reference: A Comprehensive Framework for LD Determination.*